GREAT CLASSICS OF THE SILVER SCREEN

GREAT CLASSICS OF THE SILVER SCREEN

Fifty years of the Great Classics of the Silver Screen recalled with key shots, brief resumé of the story, screen credits and background details of what went on behind the scenes of twenty-nine movie classics.

Edited by Ann Lloyd

Galahad Books - New York

Title page: RKO's poster for *King Kong*, 1933

© 1982 Orbis Publishing Limited, London
Published by Galahad Books
95 Madison Avenue
New York, New York 10016

ISBN: 0-88365-631-0

Printed in Italy

Many of the illustrations come from stills issued to
publicize films made or distributed by the
following companies: Allied Artists, Charles
Chaplin, Cinedis, Cineguild, Cocinor, Columbia,
Europa Film, London Films Mercury Productions,
MGM, Mosfilm, Paramount, Pathé-Cinéma, RKO,
20th Century-Fox, United Artists, Universal,
Warner Brothers.
Although every effort is being made to trace the
present copyright holders, we apologize in
advance for any unintentional omission or neglect
and will be pleased to insert the appropriate
acknowledgment to companies or individuals in
any subsequent edition of this publication.

Acknowledgments: Kevin Brownlow Collection,
Kingsley Canham, Peter Cowie, Greg Edwards
Archive, Joel Finler Collection, Ronald Grant
Archive, Kobal Collection, Tom Milne, National
Film Archive, David Robinson, Bob Willoughby
Collection.

CONTENTS

The Jazz Singer

Directed by Alan Crosland, 1927
Prod co: Warner Brothers. **sc:** Al Cohn, adapted from Samson Raphaelson's stage play *The Jazz Singer* (New York 1925). **titles:** Jack Jarmuth. **photo:** Hal Mohr. **ed:** Harold McCord. **mus dir:** Louis (Lou) Silvers. **songs:** 'Mammy', by Sam Lewis, Joe Young, Walter Davidson; 'Toot, Toot, Tootsie, Goodbye', by Gus Kahn, Ernie Erdman, Dan Russo; 'Dirty Hands, Dirty Face', by Edgar Leslie, Grant Clarke, Al Jolson, Jimmy Monaco; 'Blue Skies', by Irving Berlin; 'Mother, I Still Have You', by Al Jolson, Louis Silvers; Jolson also sings the Jewish chant, *Kol Nidre*. The background music includes the melodies of 'Sidewalks of New York', 'My Gal Sal', 'In the Good Old Summer Time', 'Waiting for the Robert E. Lee', 'If a Girl Like You Loved a Boy Like Me'. **sd:** George R. Groves, Vitaphone on disc. **ass dir:** Gordon Hollingshead. **r/t:** 90 min. New York premiere, 6 Oct 1927.
Cast: Al Jolson (*Jakie Rabinowitz/Jack Robin*), May McAvoy (*Mary Dale*), Warner Oland (*Cantor Rabinowitz*), Eugenie Besserer (*Sara Rabinowitz*), Bobby Gordon (*Jakie, aged 13*), Otto Lederer (*Moisha Yudelson*), Cantor Josef Rosenblatt (*himself*), Richard Tucker (*Harry Lee*), Nat Carr (*Levi*), William Demarest (*Buster Billings*), Anders Randolf (*Dillings*), Will Walling (*doctor*), Roscoe Karns (*the agent*), Myrna Loy (*chorus girl*).

Warner Bros. Supreme Triumph
AL JOLSON
THE JAZZ SINGER
price 25 cents

For the lead in their first sound feature film Warners hired Al Jolson, then vaudeville's biggest star. Jolson had not starred in *The Jazz Singer* on stage. It was George Jessel who triumphed in the leading role of the play on Broadway – and indeed Jessel was announced as the star of the film, and arrived in Hollywood on May 28, 1927. Yet only a week later Warners gave the role to Jolson.

Various reasons were offered for Warners' change of mind; part of the explanation, no doubt, was that Warners had noted the significantly warmer response of audiences to a synchronized short with Jolson than to a Jessel short which appeared with it.

The Jazz Singer was an intimate story about the conflict between family tradition and the call of the theatre in the life of a cantor's son, Jakie Rabinowitz, alias Jack Robin. The plot derived from Jolson's own life story and he introduced into the film songs he had already made famous on the stage.

The major part of the film was shot as a silent, with separate musical accompaniment, but Jolson's songs were synchronously recorded. The film caused a sensation, however, with the two sequences in which Jack (Jolson) breaks into speech. He first addresses the nightclub audience as they applaud his song: 'Wait a minute, wait a minute,' he tells them, 'you ain't heard nothin' yet'. Later he sings for his mother, and with the words 'Did you like that, Mama?' he launches into improvised conversation. This unprecedented use of natural dialogue was a staggering box-office success.

Viewed today the melodrama and the mother-love theme are antiquated; but given Alan Crosland's effective direction, the story is still compelling. The musical score is an odd pot-pourri of melodies from such heterogeneous sources as Tchaikowsky, traditional Hebrew music and popular ballads, but it is dramatically ingenious. The characters are given individual musical themes, and musical effects are skilfully edited and overlapped.

For Jolson *The Jazz Singer* was the greatest personal triumph of his career. For the film industry, it was proof that sound had come to stay.
DAVID ROBINSON

Alan Crosland
Who today remembers Alan Crosland? Yet he directed the first film with 'built-in' music and the first feature film that talked

Between two car crashes (one that nearly killed him in 1925 and the fatal one in 1936) Alan Crosland's major contribution to film history was his direction of the first two Vitaphone features in 1926 and 1927. But Crosland belongs to the silent era as unmistakably as D. W.

Griffith and, like Griffith, was fond of theatrical melodramas, believing that the object of a successful film was to transport its audience from the mundane reality of life. In other words, he made hokum. Hokum was the word applied to pictures like *The Jazz Singer* – essentially a fairy-tale film but one that still packs an emotional punch.

Crosland came into movies via journalism and stage acting, beginning his career with Edison in 1912. After a spell with Selznick in 1919, Crosland was signed by William Randolph Hearst to direct lavish, expensive costume epics (such as *The Enemies of Women*, 1923).

In 1925 he joined Warners and applied his experience of costume pictures to *Don Juan* (1926) where Mary Astor, one of the stars, remembered Crosland as a relaxed, easy-going director. The film was basically a garnish of sophistication on the familiar raw hokum.

Renewing his partnership with John Barrymore, on whom he modelled himself, Crosland made *The Beloved Rogue* (1927) – his finest surviving film. He never rose to the level of Griffith or DeMille, but he did understand the mechanics of sound better than many of his contemporaries.

Crosland was capable of imaginative flights of fantasy when provided with stronger material, and deserves to be remembered as more than just the man who made *The Jazz Singer*.
KEVIN BROWNLOW

Filmography
1917 Kidnapped; Chris and the Wonderful Lamp; Light in Darkness; Knights of the Square Table/The Grail; The Little Chevalier; Friends, Romans and Leo (short); The Apple-Tree Girl; The Story That the Keg Told Me. **'18** The Unbeliever; The Whirlpool; The Country Cousin. **'20** Greater Than Fame; Youthful Folly; The Flapper; Broadway and Home; The Point of View. **'21** Worlds Apart; Is Life Worth Living?; Room and Board. **'22** Why Announce Your Marriage? (+ co-sc); Shadows of the Sea; The Face in the Fog; The Prophet's Paradise; Slim Shoulders; The Snitching Hour. **'23** The Enemies of Women. **'24** Under the Red Robe; Three Weeks (GB: The Romance of a Queen); Miami; Unguarded Women; Sinners in Heaven. **'25** Contraband; Bobbed Hair; Compromise. **'26** Don Juan; When a Man Loves (GB: His Lady). **'27** The Beloved Rogue; Old San Francisco; The Jazz Singer. **'28** Glorious Betsy; The Scarlet Lady (GB: The Scarlet Woman). **'29** On With the Show; General Crack. **'30** The Furies; Song of the Flame; Viennese Nights; Big Boy; Captain Thunder. **'31** Children of Dreams; The Silver Lining (+ prod) (GB: Thirty Days). **'32** Week-ends Only. **'33** Massacre. **'34** The Personality Kid; Midnight Alibi; The Case of the Howling Dog. **'35** The White Cockatoo; It Happened in New York; Mister Dynamite; Lady Tubbs; King Solomon of Broadway; The Great Impersonation.

1

2

Cantor Rabinowitz is furious to find his son, Jakie, singing in a bar when he should be in the synagogue. The Cantor beats him and he runs away.

Years later, Jakie, now known as Jack Robin, is heard singing at Coffee Dan's nightclub (1) by actress Mary Dale who offers to help his career.

Jack is soon touring with Mary's theatre company, but sadly they must part for she has accepted a role on Broadway. In Chicago Jack's memories are stirred by the singing of a cantor. Then Jack learns that he too has got a spot in a Broadway revue.

In New York Jack is reunited with Mama, but the Cantor is shocked to hear his son's music and banishes him again (2).

Jack arrives at the rehearsals and realizes that it was Mary who arranged his big chance. Meanwhile, the Cantor falls ill and Jack finds himself torn between duty to his father and the show. Mama comes to appeal to him to come home – but sees he belongs to the stage (3).

However Jack relents and makes his dying father happy by singing *Kol Nidre* in the synagogue (4). The show eventually goes on and when Mama comes to see it, Jack croons 'My Mammy' to her (5).

3

4

5

Directed by Lewis Milestone, 1930
Prod co: Universal. **prod:** Carl Laemmle Jr. **sc:** Del Andrews, Maxwell Anderson, George Abbott, from the novel *Im Westen Nichts Neues* by Erich Maria Remarque. **dial:** Maxwell Anderson, George Abbott, C. Gardner Sullivan. **dial dir:** George Cukor. **titles:** Walter Anthony. **photo:** Arthur Edeson. **sp eff photo:** Frank H. Booth. **ed:** Edgar Adams, Milton Carruth, Maurice Pivar. **art dir:** Charles D. Hall, W. R. Schmitt. **sync/mus:** David Broekman. **rec sup:** C. Roy Hunter. **sd:** William W. Hedgecock. **sd sys:** Movietone. **ass dir:** Nate Watt. **r/t:** 138 minutes. New York premiere, 28 April 1930.
Cast: Lew Ayres (*Paul Baumer*), Louis Wolheim (*Katczinsky*), John Wray (*Himmelstoss*), George 'Slim' Summerville (*Tjaden*), Raymond Griffith (*Gerard Duval*), Russell Gleason (*Müller*), William Bakewell (*Albert*), Scott Kolk (*Leer*), Walter Rogers (*Bohm*), Ben Alexander (*Kemmerich*), Owen Davis Jr (*Peter*), Beryl Mercer (*Paul's mother* – sound version), ZaSu Pitts (*Paul's mother* – silent version), Edwin Maxwell (*Paul's father*), Harold Goodwin (*Detering*), Marion Clayton (*Paul's sister*), Richard Alexander (*Westhus*), G. Pat Collins (*Lieutenant Bertinck*), Yola D'Avril (*Suzanne*), Poupée Andriot, Renée Damonde (*French girls*), Arnold Lucy (*Kantorek*), William Irving (*Ginger*), Edmund Breese (*Herr Meyer*), Heinie Conklin (*Hammacher*), Bertha Mann (*Sister*), Bodil Rosing (*Wachter*), Joan Marsh (*poster girl*), Tom London (*orderly*), Vincent Barnett (*cook*), Fred Zinnemann (*man*).

Our bodies are earth and our thoughts are clay and we sleep and eat with death

Erich Maria Remarque wrote *Im Westen Nichts Neues* to free himself from his memory of the Great War and from 'my thoughts and those of my companions'. Like the leading character in the novel, the author was one of a class of 18-year-olds who enlisted in the infantry and suffered the brutalities of life in the trenches. The book was a best-seller. Soon after it appeared in the United States, the rights were snapped up by Carl Laemmle, head of Universal. Laemmle originally intended to use the story for a silent movie, and a silent version with synchronized music exists – running a reel longer than the complete talkie copy and with ZaSu Pitts in the role of Mrs Baumer instead of Beryl Mercer, who played the part in the sound film. (Perhaps Miss Mercer's stage experience was thought to fit her better for talkies.)

Lewis Milestone set himself uncompromisingly to reproduce the realism of the novel. It is arguable that no film – whether fiction or fact – has given so vivid an account of the physical actuality of World War I; and fragments of *All Quiet* have frequently turned up in later compilations, credited as documentary.

The battle scenes were shot on an area of almost 1000 acres on the Irvine Ranch, 69 miles south-east of Los Angeles. Over 5 miles of water

pipes were laid to provide the authentic water-logged appearance of the battlefields. And 2 miles of road were built for the operation of Universal's high new camera crane which was assigned to the picture. In all, 35 different sets were built for the film – those representing front-line France being destined for destruction during filming.

Unerringly, Milestone reconciled the realism of the setting with the deliberately lyrical style of the dialogue: 'Our bodies are earth and our thoughts are clay, and we sleep and eat with death'. He also blended the extreme stylization of some performances with the easy naturalism of Louis Wolheim (Katczinsky) and Slim Summerville (Tjaden).

Milestone used his facilities with incomparable flair. He brought all the fluidity of silent films to the camera – which freely tracked and panned and soared over the battlefields or the little German town from which the hero and his schoolboy friends march out to war – and to the editing. At the same time Milestone imaginatively explored the possibilities of sound, from the beginning where the bellicose harangues of the schoolteacher are drowned by the noise of a band outside, to the haunting echoes of the battlefield as the cry of 'Mind the wire' goes down the line.   DAVID ROBINSON

At the outset of World War I a group of German boys leave their desks for the army, inspired by the marching soldiers in the streets (1) and by the uplifting rhetoric of their schoolmaster. Only one wavers but he too is eventually persuaded (2). Sent to the front, their illusions are shattered by the cynical stoicism of seasoned soldiers (3) and by their own first experiences under fire (4). They share the terror and exhaustion of constant fighting as well as the bewilderment of watching their schoolfriends die (5) on the battlefield.

The central character is Paul Baumer. His first experience of killing a man, face to face, is traumatic (6): in other circumstances the Frenchman could have been a friend and comrade rather than the enemy.

After being wounded, Paul is sent home on leave to find a world with which he now has little contact. False romantic ideas of war still persist in the school and among the belligerent old men in the beer cellars (7).

Almost with relief he returns to the front. A few old comrades are still alive in his unit but it is mostly filled with new recruits – as young and green as he was once, not so many months ago.

Some time later Paul is peering through the loophole of his trench (8) when he sees a butterfly. He reaches out to catch it (9). A French sniper takes aim. Paul's hand falls limp.

Across the corpse-strewn fields of France march columns of ghostly soldiers – accusation in their eyes (10).

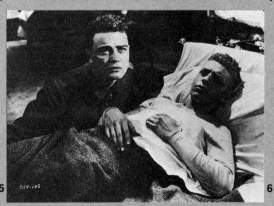

GRAND HOTEL

HOLLYWOOD'S FIRST ALL-STAR SPECTACULAR

Herman Shumlin, an experienced Broadway producer. He stipulated that the film should not be shown until the play closed or until 15 months after its opening in November 1930. This left MGM plenty of time to work out a script, assign the artists and build up publicity for the film.

Fejos did not direct *Grand Hotel*. Thalberg tested him for it by assigning him to *The Great Lover* (1932) but then withdrew him – and that was the end of Fejos's more-than-promising Hollywood career. Thalberg next considered using Lewis Milestone, fresh from his success with *All Quiet on the Western Front* (1930), but eventually decided on Edmund Goulding, an English-born director and former writer who had made several films for MGM. The $700,000 budget was well above average but not unprecedented: what made the film an unusual production was its galaxy of stars.

Fans camped outside the Palace Theatre the night before *Grand Hotel* opened in London and contemporary critics were delighted with the film. Mordaunt Hall, writing in the *New York Times*, said, 'It is a production thoroughly worthy of all the talk it has created.' C.A. Lejeune wrote in *The Observer*:

'To see Garbo in a fine new freedom of mood – even her poses have broken down their old contours – balanced by a Barrymore who has forgotten his mannerisms; to see Wallace Beery in full control of his vast ebullience, and Crawford turning her slick youth to grim and logical purpose; to see Lionel Barrymore suddenly towering . . . over the rest of the cast – to be given all this in one film, is good measure for any audience, but a measure that reserves its special bouquet for the movie connoisseur.'

Garbo's performance – it is here she sobs 'I want to be alone' – was judged flawless by most contemporary critics: '. . . the essence of a fragrant and exquisite disappointment' (*Arts Weekly*, 1932). We now know she can do better, and it has been suggested since that Joan Crawford steals the film from her. Both are more effective than their male co-stars: John Barrymore's account of his role now seems particularly specious. Lew Stone and Jean Hersholt, two stalwart MGM character actors cast in minor roles, provide more than adequate support for the stars, however.

The fates of the characters devised by Miss Baum and MGM's scenarists are perhaps less important than the film's atmosphere – which was largely created by Cedric Gibbons's art deco interiors. Above all, Goulding and MGM sought to convey a 'German' feel – though it is only with difficulty today that we can imagine ourselves in Berlin. The brittle, detached quality borrowed from the German cinema, which once seemed a virtue when most films were sentimental, sits oddly on this wholly American product, and *Grand Hotel* now appears rather dusty.

DAVID SHIPMAN

Few all-star specials had emerged from Hollywood before MGM's *Grand Hotel* brought together Greta Garbo, Joan Crawford, Wallace Beery and the Barrymore brothers to portray characters whose lives are dramatically interwoven as they pass through a stylish Berlin hotel. The film popularized the multi-stranded, star-laden movie – it was immediately followed by the Studio's *Dinner at Eight* (1933) which, in its souvenir programme, claimed *twelve* stars.

Menschen im Hotel (People in a Hotel), the novel on which *Grand Hotel* was based, was published in 1929. It followed a number of cross-section studies of Berlin low-life, by painters, cartoonists, novelists and film-makers, that were very popular in Germany in the Twenties. Vicki Baum, author of *Menschen im Hotel*, had worked as a parlour-maid for six weeks in a Berlin hotel in order to get authentic material for her book.

The novel was an instant success and a dramatization appeared on the Berlin stage in 1930. This was *not* a success, but MGM's property-finder, Kate Corbaley, read a short newspaper article about the play and sent for a copy. Paul Fejos, a newly-contracted director, was the first to read it and had the studio pursue the stage and screen rights, only to find they had been sold by Miss Baum to an agent, Dr Edmund Pawker, for $4500. He had recently arrived in New York and was to co-produce the play with Harry Moses, a manufacturer of ladies' underwear. Mr Moses had seen the play performed in Berlin and considered it an ideal property for launching his wife on a theatrical career. MGM secured the film rights for a $15,000 contribution to the New York production, with an equal amount from Moses.

After one rehearsal Mrs Moses dropped out. MGM then brought in

Directed by Edmund Goulding, 1932
Prod co: MGM. **dir:** Edmund Goulding. **sc:** William A. Drake, and Frances Marion (uncredited), adapted from novel *Menschen im Hotel* by Vicki Baum. **photo:** William Daniels. **ed:** Blanche Sewell. **art dir:** Cedric Gibbons. **cost:** Adrian. **mus:** Herbert Stothart. **rec eng:** Douglas Shearer. **ass dir:** Charles Dorian. **r/t:** 112 min. New York premiere, 12 April 1932.
Cast: Greta Garbo (*Grusinskaya*), John Barrymore (*Baron Felix von Gaigern*), Joan Crawford (*Flaemmchen*), Wallace Beery (*Preysing*), Lionel Barrymore (*Otto Kringelein*), Lewis Stone (*Dr Otternschlag*), Jean Hersholt (*Senf*), Robert McWade (*Meierheim*), Purnell D. Pratt (*Zinnowitz*), Ferdinand Gottschalk (*Pimenov*), Rafaela Ottiano (*Suzette*), Tully Marshall (*Gerstenkorn*), Morgan Wallace (*Schweinke, the chauffeur*), Frank Conroy (*Rohna*), Murray Kinnell (*Schweimann*), Edwin Maxwell (*Dr Waitz*), Mary Carlisle (*honeymooner*), John Davidson (*hotel manager*), Sam McDaniel (*bartender*), Rolfe Sedan, Herbert Evans (*clerks*), Lee Phelps (*extra*).

1

2

3

Grusinskaya, a ballerina whose popularity has waned, books in at the hotel (1) and is soon seen languishing in her room. She will not wear her pearls, believing that they have brought her bad luck (2), and the impoverished Baron von Gaigern sets out to steal them.

Meanwhile, Preysing, who has checked in to settle a business deal upon which his survival depends, attracts Flaemmchen, one of the hotel's stenographers. She has decided there are quicker ways to a mink coat than taking shorthand.

Grusinskaya, still in her tutu after another unhappy performance (3), interrupts the Baron who has had to hide quickly in her room after taking the pearls. Seeing that she is seriously contemplating suicide he hastily comes out of hiding. He explains his presence by claiming to be an admirer but soon realizes he is in love with her (4).

He returns the pearls, she falls in love with him and they plan to go away to start a new life.

The dying Kringelein, Preysing's former clerk, has befriended the Baron but the latter steals from him – once again returning his prize, this time from remorse.

Desperate for money, the Baron then attempts to rob Preysing who catches him in the act and kills him with the telephone (5). Flaemmchen, who has been with Preysing (6), tells Kringelein and he takes revenge on his former employer, calling the police to arrest Preysing (7). Kringelein and Flaemmchen, now thrown together, discuss their future and decide to leave for Paris.

Grusinskaya leaves the hotel happily, still expecting to meet the Baron. The hotel doctor checks in at the desk that morning but there is no news for him and he complains that nothing ever happens at the hotel.

4

5

6

7

The Private Life of Henry VIII

Directed by Alexander Korda, 1933

Prod co: London Film Productions. **prod:** Alexander Korda. **dir:** Alexander Korda. **sc:** Arthur Wimperis. **story/dial:** Lajos Biro and Arthur Wimperis. **photo:** Georges Périnal. **ed:** Harold Young, Stephen Harrison. **des:** Vincent Korda. **cost:** John Armstrong. **mus:** Kurt Schroeder. **song:** 'What Shall I Do for Love' by King Henry VIII, sung by Binnie Barnes. **sd:** A.W. Watkins. **r/t:** 96 minutes. London premiere, 17 August 1933.

Cast: Charles Laughton (*Henry VIII*), Robert Donat (*Culpeper*), Lady Tree (*Henry's Old Nurse*), Binnie Barnes (*Catherine Howard*), Elsa Lanchester (*Anne of Cleves*), Merle Oberon (*Anne Boleyn*), Wendy Barrie (*Jane Seymour*), Everley Gregg (*Catherine Parr*), Franklyn Dyall (*Cromwell*), Miles Mander (*Wriothesly*), Claude Allister (*Cornell*), John Loder (*Thomas Peynell*), Lawrence Hanray (*Cranmer*), William Austin (*Duke of Cleves*), John Turnbull (*Holbein*), Frederick Culley (*Duke of Norfolk*), Gibb McLaughlin (*French executioner*), Sam Livesey (*English executioner*), Judy Kelly (*Lady Rochford*).

The Hungarian Alexander Korda had a favourite story about how he got the idea for *The Private Life of Henry VIII*. Shortly after his arrival in England, he was travelling in a London Taxi when he heard the driver singing, 'I'm Henery the Eighth, I Am'. Misunderstanding the old song about a widow's eight marriages – all to men called Henry ('And every one was an Henery, she wouldn't have a Willie or a Sam') – Korda reflected that Henry VIII must be a figure of wide popular appeal.

However, studio after studio failed to share his enthusiasm and rejected his idea. Korda finally obtained enough backing from the United Artists Company to start filming. Such was the belief in the project, that many of the crew and cast agreed to wait until its completion before being fully paid. Eventually enough money was found to finish the film. It had been shot in five weeks for the modest sum of £60,000. Korda's faith in the film was soon justified. The script had a daring which might not have been possible under an English director – and was the first ever to be published in book form. The cast displayed an assurance still not common in the British cinema. Georges Périnal was the cameraman and the visual images were beautiful: the outdoor scenes clear and brilliant, the interiors rich with velvety darkness. Above all the film had an irreverence new to the cinema. Surprised critics hailed it as a cinematic event – the best production, they said, to come out of a British studio.

Of course there were dissonant voices. One pedantic authority on armour and costume complained that Henry wore his spurs 'like a cowboy', with the buckles on the inside of his feet instead of the outside. In 1936 James Agate was saying that Charles Laughton had 'permitted himself to label a bundle of buffooneries "Henry VIII"'. Despite criticism, however, the piece captured not only the British but also the American public. For the first time a British-made film was a very big commercial success in the USA.

The attitude of disrespect no doubt made the film a sensation. A beautiful woman (Anne Boleyn, played by Merle Oberon), who is also a queen, is to be beheaded: the victim is bravely resigned, and executioner whets his axe – and a spectator in the crowd grumbles that she can't see the block. Another woman is crowned, then another: for a while no more heads are cut off. But in the royal kitchens servants can still make a joke of the previous lethal 'preliminaries' to a wedding: 'chop and change', is one fellow's waggish comment.

Yet the light, flippant handling of the story is not allowed to obscure the drama. Jealousy and passion are there. The King is besotted with Catherine Howard and he genuinely suffers when his ministers convince him that she has been unfaithful to him. And behind the scenes torture lurks; the threat of it induces Catherine's waiting-women to betray her. But the treatment remains ironic: the King, for all his authority is mocked; Anne of Cleves makes a fool of him; Catherine Parr bullies him in his old age.

Sometimes the abrupt changes of mood have a tastlessness for which the virtues of the film – its wit, its entertaining emphasis on royal follies and frailties – fail to compensate. That the piece nevertheless achieves a kind of unity is largely owing to the performance of Charles Laughton. He was already a distinguished actor when he took the role (which brought him an Oscar). But although he went on to a score of successes, it is still his portrait of Henry VIII – arrogant, lecherous, vengeful, finally absurd – which comes first to mind. Especially memorable is the bedroom scene between him and Anne of Cleves (played by his real-life wife, Elsa Lanchester), who on their wedding night evades the King's unwelcome physical attentions by engaging and beating him in a game of cards.

The film's popularity in the USA was perhaps something of a fluke – the outcome of a chance combination of a favourite leading player, an impudent handling of British history, a strain of vulgarity pleasing to spectators who liked to think an English king had no table-manners. Time has softened the vulgarities, turning them into the mildest of sick jokes. The irreverence persists: Henry wrangling with his barber, Henry challenged by his own guard as he creeps upstairs on an amorous nocturnal expedition. And irreverence it was which, in 1933, endeared the film to a public ready to enjoy a joke at the expense of royalty: especially British royalty.

DILYS POWELL

Below: Korda supervises the shooting of the famous banquet scene with Laughton at the table

1

2

3

4

5

6

The King (1) has divorced Catherine of Aragon, and, as the film begins, is ridding himself of his second wife, Anne Boleyn. Nervously, but with dignity, she prepares for execution (2); the waiting crowds treat the occasion as an enjoyable outing.

Meanwhile Jane Seymour waits excitedly to become Henry's third wife. Her success is brief. Out hunting, the King learns that he has a son (3); but the Queen dies. He is reluctant to marry again, but popular sentiment persuades him to consider Anne of Cleves as his fourth wife (4). Anne, however, decides to make herself unattractive to the King. The marriage night is spent playing cards (5); she wins the game and her release from wedlock. Henry is next introduced to Catherine Howard by Thomas Culpeper (6) and falls hopelessly in love (7). Ambitious to be Queen, Catherine marries Henry, but in secret she and Culpeper are lovers. Her adultery is discovered, and again crowds gather to see a queen beheaded. Finally a sixth wife, Catherine Parr, bullies the King, supervising his food and drink. When we last see him he is a henpecked, shambling old man, guzzling behind his wife's back (8).

7

8

KING KONG

King Kong is the most potent myth that the cinema has given to the 20th century. It is the archetypal legend of Beauty and the Beast: after Kong's death, a policeman triumphantly tells Denham, 'Well, the planes got him'. 'No', Denham replies sadly, 'it wasn't the airplanes. It was Beauty killed the Beast.' The giant ape is an authentic figure of tragedy, cruel as Timon, strong as Samson, jealous as Othello, cursed as Orestes and as vulnerable as them all.

Appropriately for a legend, the authorship of *Kong* is not entirely clear. The idea seems to have begun with Merian C. Cooper, who had become fascinated, while on safari, with the habits of the gorilla, and wished to make a film in which a great ape would terrorize New York.

Cooper and Ernest B. Schoedsack, co-producer and director of the film, had previously made two travel documentaries together, *Grass* (1926) and *Chang* (1927), and two narrative films one of which, *The Four Feathers* (1929), starred Fay Wray, Kong's leading lady. In 1932 David O. Selznick brought Cooper to RKO, where there was a project for a film using Willis J. O'Brien, who had done the animation work on the 1925 version of *The Lost World*. Cooper and O'Brien made some test sequences for *King Kong*, which encouraged RKO to embark on a project which, at $650,000, was very costly for those times. Edgar Wallace, under contract to the studio, was commissioned to write the screenplay, but died before the film was properly under way, and it is still uncertain how much the famous English thriller writer contributed to the finished film. His daughter, in a letter to *The Times* in 1978, suggested that the whole conception was his; but Fay Wray recalls:

'I looked up Wallace's own version of the story recently, and it has different characters, different names, different scenes from the ones I knew in the film.' Cooper and Schoedsack in later interviews confirmed Miss Wray's opinion. The writers actually credited on the film are James Creelman and Ruth Rose (Mrs Schoedsack).

In any event, though the film is a masterpiece of narrative structure, the writing is less important than its plastic qualities. Once under way *King Kong* often looks like a silent film: the action is essentially visual, and complemented by Max Steiner's highly dramatic musical score. Its pictorial qualities too are notable: Skull Island might have come from some nightmare etching by Gustave Doré.

Above all, credit is due to Willis O'Brien's animation. Kong and the other fantastic creatures, like the pterodactyl he fights, were three-dimensional models, not more than 16 inches high, which were filmed using stop-action photography. Between every frame of film, the camera was stopped and the eyes and the limbs of the figures reposed, barely perceptibly, to give an impression of lively, realistic movement when the finished film was projected. Generally the animated figures were combined with shots of the actors in subsequent process work; but for some close-ups – for example where Fay Wray has to lie in the monster's paw – huge working models of parts of the body were made.

Technical qualities alone cannot explain the instant hold that *King Kong* took on the imagination of the world, and which it continues to exert. (Kong himself was publicized at the time as the 'Eighth Wonder of the World'.) It is myth and it is dream: the apparition of Kong in the jungle, or the great eye peering through a Manhattan window, are elemental nightmares. The film enshrines the essential eroticism of the Beauty and the Beast myth.

Moreover the film appeared at the height of the Depression: Ann Darrow is first discovered starving near a bread queue and stealing an apple. It may be significant that the 1977 remake came at a comparable moment of economic uncertainty. Was there some deeper satisfaction to audiences in watching Kong's triumphant destruction of that urban jungle of steel and glass which had brought betrayal?

DAVID ROBINSON

Directed by Ernest B. Schoedsack, Merian C. Cooper, 1933
Prod co: RKO-Radio Pictures. **prod**: Ernest B. Schoedsack, Merian C. Cooper. **sc**: James Creelman, Ruth Rose, from a story by Merian C. Cooper, Edgar Wallace. **photo**: Edward Lindon, Vernon Walker, J.O. Taylor. **sp eff**: Willis O'Brien. **ed**: Ted Cheesman. **art dir**: Carroll Clark, Alfred Herman, Mario Larrinaga, Byron L. Crabbe. **mus**: Max Steiner. **sd**: E.A. Woolcott. **sd eff**: Murray Spivak. **prod ass**: Archie S. Marshek, Walter Daniels. **r/t**: 99 minutes. New York premiere 2 March 1933.
Cast: Fay Wray (*Ann Darrow*), Robert Armstrong (*Carl Denham*), Frank Reicher (*Englehorn*), Bruce Cabot (*Driscoll*), Sam Hardy (*Weston*), Noble Johnson (*native chief*), James Flavin (*lieutenant*), Victor Wong (*Lumpy*), Steve Clemento (*witchdoctor*).

1

2

3

4

5

7

8

Carl Denham, a film producer, selects an unknown and impoverished girl, Ann Darrow, to play in a mysterious film to be made on a remote tropical location with the forbidding name of Skull Island. Soon after their arrival (1), Ann is seized by natives (2), who need a beautiful girl to placate their god, Kong. Helpless, Ann is bound to two great pillars (3).

At last Kong, a monstrous ape, appears (4). He picks up Ann in his huge hand and carries her off into the jungle, pursued by Denham and the crew. Most of the crew are killed when Kong hurls them off a log bridge, but Denham and his assistant Driscoll rescue Ann while Kong is distracted by a fight with a pterodactyl (5).

Subdued by a gas bomb, Kong is taken to New York to be exhibited (6). He escapes, however, and wreaks terrible havoc. Snatching Ann from the window of a skyscraper, he carries her to the top of the Empire State Building (7). There the great beast is attacked by fighter planes (8) and dies riddled with machine gun bullets.

Modern Times

Directed by Charles Chaplin, 1936
Prod/sc/mus: Charles Chaplin. **photo:** Rollie Totheroh, Ira Morgan. **art dir:** Charles D. Hall, Russell Spencer. **mus dir:** Alfred Newman. **mus arr:** Edward Powell, David Raskin. **ass dir:** Carter de Haven, Henry Bergman. **r/t** 87 minutes. New York premiere, 5 February 1936.
Cast: Charles Chaplin (*Tramp*), Paulette Goddard (*working-class girl*), Henry Bergman (*café owner*), Chester Conklin (*mechanic*), Allan Garcia (*steelworks manager*), Lloyd Ingraham (*prison governor*), Louis Netheaux (*drug addict*), John Rand (*jailbird*), Stanley Sanford (*fellow conveyor-belt worker*), Hank Mann (*cellmate*), Mira McKinney (*prison chaplain's wife*), Richard Alexander (*prison chaplain*), Wilfred Lucas, Edward Kimball, Murdock McQuarry, (*fellow prisoners/workers*).

Chaplin regarded talking pictures as the ruin of 'the world's most ancient art, the art of pantomime. They annihilate the great beauty of silence'. *Modern Times* is conceived as a silent film. With the exception of the star's voice – heard for the first time on film when he sings a nonsense song – the only voices featured issue from television screens or loudspeakers. *Modern Times* was also the last appearance of Chaplin's Tramp figure – the little vagrant in a too-small Derby hat, too large boots, baggy pants, tight jacket, and a wing collar and sporty cane that proclaimed fallen gentility. This character first appeared on the screen 22 years before, in 1914, and achieved a universal acceptance such as no fictional image of a man had known before.

The film was poorly received by the critics of the time. Chaplin was charged with exceeding the proper function of the clown, of trying to set himself up as a popular philosopher. At the same time he was accused of being old-fashioned and cowardly in rejecting sound: after all, this was the era of the Marx Brothers, Mae West and W.C. Fields. In film technique, they said, he had learned little since 1914. Inevitably too, the film was charged with sinister political implications. It was banned in fascist Italy and Germany – and somewhat frowned upon in the USSR, on account of its satire on modern productivity. Protested Chaplin:

'Our only purpose was to amuse. It was just my old Charlie character in circumstances of 1936. I have no political aims whatever as an actor.'

'It started from an abstract idea, an impulse to say something about the way life is being standardized and channelized, and men turned into machines – and the way I felt about it. I knew that was what I wanted to do before I thought of any of the details.'

Chaplin's art has survived these criticisms. *Modern Times* looks perhaps even fresher today than on its original release. The film's chief quality – a characteristic of all of Chaplin's best work – is not so much its *modernity* as its *timelessness*. Chaplin's universe is not tied to a particular era, but seems to belong to all times Though the world of *Modern Times* is the world of the American Depression, its characteristics – industrial regimentation, strikes, riots, drugs, demonstrations, urban pollution, the inhuman rigidity of bureaucratic social institutions – are all relevant and vivid to us today. And at the same time as the issues still seem topical more than forty years on, so the characters and sentiments often reach back to the nineteenth century. When Chaplin speaks of poverty and vagrancy, shows the child-care men snatching a child from a slum home, or shapes his vision of Paulette Goddard's sharp-faced little waif, he looks back to *The Kid* (1921), and beyond that to his own childhood in the slums and orphanages of Victorian London.

It is a film of brilliant set pieces, in which all the technical skills Chaplin had first learned in the English music halls are brought into play. W.C. Fields intended to insult him when he called Chaplin 'the best goddammed ballet dancer in the business', but it was only the truth: the conveyor belt sequence in the opening of the film is a masterpiece of choreography. A moment's inattention to his mechanical task, when he brushes away a troublesome fly, causes chaos throughout the production line – and when finally he goes berserk, it is to dance his way into a beautiful mad ballet. demonically attacking with spanners anything that looks amenable to tightening, including the buttons of a busty lady who chances to be passing. There are comparable compositions of movement and mime in a scene where, having inadvertently swallowed a massive dose of 'joy powder', he pirouettes out of the prison dining-hall in the wake of a line of marching convicts; or in the miraculous, virtuoso sequence where he roller-skates, blindfold, on the brink of an abyss.

The full genius of Chaplin's comedy, however, appears in the scene where he obligingly picks up the red warning flag which has fallen off a passing lorry. He runs after it, quite unaware that a mass demonstration has formed up behind him. It is impossible to say whether the scene is comic or tragic. Either way, it remains one of the great symbolic representations of man as victim of his fate.

DAVID ROBINSON

16

Charlie plays a factory worker whose job is to tighten bolts of an endless series of machine parts on a moving belt (1). He is used as a guinea pig for a new aid to productivity – a machine that automatically feeds the men as they work. Finally he cracks under the strain, runs amok (2), and is sent to a mental hospital.

Discharged and part of the great army of unemployed, he helpfully picks up a red flag that has fallen from a lorry (3) – only to be arrested as a communist agitator. In prison, he accidentally averts a jailbreak and is given his freedom (4). Life outside prison is so fraught with perils, however, that he tries – vainly – to get arrested again. He attempts to take the blame when an orphaned waif, on the run from the child-care authorities, steals a loaf of bread (5). The two decide to join forces.

A job as a night watchman in a big store ends in disaster and jail again. Released, he returns to the factory, but a strike instantly puts him out of work and back on the streets. The girl is by this time a dancer in cabaret, where she finds him a job as a singing waiter. When this too ends in disaster (6), Charlie and the waif take off, the child-care men on their heels. They are last seen walking hand in hand down a country road (7).

E
LIN
OY
ERN
MES

Directed and Produced by
RLES CHAPLIN

UNITED ARTISTS

7

Alexander Nevsky

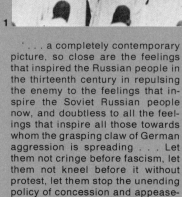

Directed by Sergei Eisenstein, 1938
Prod co: Mosfilm. **sc:** Sergei Eisenstein, Pyotr Pavlenko. **photo:** Eduard Tissé. **art dir:** Isaak Shpinel, Nikolai Solovyov, Konstantin Eliseyev, from drawings by Eisenstein. **mus:** Sergei Prokofiev. **ass dir:** Dmitri Vasiliev, Boris Ivanov, Nikolai Maslov. **r/t:** 112 minutes. Moscow premiere, 23 November 1938.
Cast: Nikolai Cherkasov (*Alexander Nevsky*), Nikolai Okhlopkov (*Vasili Buslai*), Alexander Abrikosov (*Gavrilo Olexich*), Dmitri Orlov (*Ignat*), Vasili Novikov (*Pavsha, governor of Pskov*), Vera Ivasheva (*Olga*), Nikolai Arsky (*Domash*), Varvara Massalitinova (*Amelfa*), Anna Danilova (*Vasilisa*), Vladimir Ershov (*Grand Master of the Teutonic Order*), Sergei Blinnikov (*Tverdilo*), Lev Fenin (*bishop*), I. Lagutin (*Ananias*), Naum Rogozhin (*black monk*).

Alexander Nevsky was the first film to be completed by Eisenstein since *The Old and the New* (1929) as well as being his first sound film. It offered an opportunity for the realization of the ideas on sound expressed in the 1928 *Declaration* by Eisenstein, Pudovkin and Aleksandrov. In this the authors warn that a mere:

'. . . *adhesion* of sound to pieces of montage reinforces their inertia.

'*Only a contrapuntal use* of sound in relation to the piece of visual montage offers new possibilities for the development and perfection of montage. *The first experiments with sound must be directed towards a sharp contrast between it and the visual images*. And only such a "storm" will produce the sensation needed to create a new *orchestral counterpoint* of visual and sound images.'

This concept of 'orchestral counterpoint', is exemplified in the Battle on the Ice sequence by the interaction between Eisenstein's powerful imagery and Prokofiev's dramatic musical score.

Alexander Nevsky was also the film that marked Eisenstein's return to official respectability. After *October* (1927) and *The Old and the New* Eisenstein had gone abroad, but his film projects there remained unfinished. Returning to the USSR, he fell foul of Boris Shumyatsky, administrative 'tsar' of the Soviet film industry. When he was eventually permitted to begin filming *Bezhin Meadow* the project was halted by Shumyatsky in March 1937, after two million roubles had already been spent on its production. This was an expensive mistake, not only for Soviet film art, but also for Shumyatsky: he was purged as a 'captive of the saboteurs' in January 1938.

This gave Eisenstein his opportunity. He began filming *Alexander Nevsky* on June 5 and completed it on November 7. The film had its premiere a fortnight later. In the process of its rapid editing Eisenstein fell asleep one evening. While the director slept, an incomplete print was removed to the Kremlin and shown to Stalin, who was eager to see it. He liked what he saw, and this made it difficult for Eisenstein to add the missing sequences. Thus his most successful film remained for him the most unsatisfactory – at least from an artistic point of view. At the time, Eisenstein noted:

'*Nevsky* is brazenly effective despite *itself*. *Everyone* can see its staginess *above all*, its length, the rhythmic breaks and failures. *Everyone* can see them, not just the specialists . . . And it is effective *nonetheless*. Why? . . . There's only a single thought and everything revolves around a *single* thought. There's not a word, a remark, an episode or a scene where the dialogue and the plot are not concerned with the enemy and the need to defeat him.'

The story of the Russian people's successful struggle against the Teutonic Knights was an allegorical warning to the Nazis. Alexander's final address to the liberated citizens of Pskov renders this explicit:

'Go and tell all in foreign parts that Rus lives. Let people come to us as guests without fear. But he who comes with the sword shall perish by the sword. On this Rus stands and will stand forever!'

Alexander Nevsky was, in Eisenstein's words:

'. . . a completely contemporary picture, so close are the feelings that inspired the Russian people in the thirteenth century in repulsing the enemy to the feelings that inspire the Soviet Russian people now, and doubtless to all the feelings that inspire all those towards whom the grasping claw of German aggression is spreading . . . Let them not cringe before fascism, let them not kneel before it without protest, let them stop the unending policy of concession and appeasement towards this insatiable mon-

2

3

ster. Let the sceptics remember that there is no force of gloom and darkness that could stand against the combined efforts of all that is best, healthiest, most progressive and forward-looking in mankind.'

The article in which Eisenstein penned these words was called 'Patriotism Is My Theme': it remained unpublished in the USSR because, in August 1939, the Nazi–Soviet Pact was signed. The film no longer served a useful political purpose and was removed from circulation. But by then both

the director and Nikolai Cherkasov, who played Alexander, had been awarded the Order of Lenin, the highest order that the Soviet Union can bestow.

Following the German invasion of the USSR on June 22, 1941, *Alexander Nevsky* was re-released. It is a tribute to both Eisenstein and his politically most successful film that the Soviet government soon instituted a new battle honour for bravery at the front – the Order of Alexander Nevsky.

RICHARD TAYLOR

Thirteenth-century Russia is laid waste by the Mongol hordes from the East, while the Teutonic Knights (1) invade from the West, capturing the ancient city of Pskov and committing atrocities against the population (2). The men of Novgorod call on Alexander Nevsky to lead the Russian forces. The people take arms (3).

On the eve of battle, Ignat entertains the men with the tale of the hare and the vixen: as the hare cannot outpace her, he runs between two closely planted tree

trunks. Following him, the vixen is trapped and the hare deflowers her. This tale inspires Alexander's battle strategy. The Russian armies lie in wait (4), luring the Teutonic Knights (5) onto the frozen surface of Lake Peipus (6); the weight of their armour cracks the ice and they drown in the freezing water. This is the famous Battle on the Ice.

At the head of his victorious forces, Alexander enters Pskov to be fêted by the population (7). Russia is free.

7

6

1

Directed by John Ford 1940

Prod co: 20th Century-Fox. **prod:** Darryl F. Zanuck. **assoc prod/sc:** Nunnally Johnson, from the novel by John Steinbeck. **photo:** Gregg Toland. **ed:** Robert Simpson. **art dir:** Richard Day, Mark Lee Kirk, Thomas Little. **mus:** Alfred Newman. **sd:** George Leverett, Roger Heman. **sd eff ed:** Robert Parrish. **ass dir:** Edward O'Fearna. **r/t:** 129 minutes. New York premiere, 24 January 1940.

Cast: Henry Fonda (*Tom Joad*), Jane Darwell (*Ma Joad*), John Carradine (*Casy*), Charley Grapewin (*Grampa Joad*), Dorris Bowdon (*Rosaharn*), Russell Simpson (*Pa Joad*), O.Z. Whitehead (*Al*), John Qualen (*Muley*), Eddie Quillan (*Connie*), Zeffie Tilbury (*Grandma Joad*), Frank Sully (*Noah*), Frank Darlen (*Uncle John*), Darryl Hickman (*Winfield*), Shirley Mills (*Ruth Joad*), Grant Mitchell (*guardian*), Ward Bond (*policeman*), Frank Faylen (*Tim*), Joe Sawyer (*accountant*), Harry Tyler (*Bert*), Charles B. Middleton (*conductor*), John Arledge (*Davis*), Hollis Jewell (*Muley's son*), Paul Guilfoyle (*Floyd*), Charles D. Brown (*Wilkie*), Roger Imhof (*Thomas*), William Pawley (*Bill*), Arthur Aylesworth (*Father*), Charles Tannen (*Joe*), Selmar Jackson (*inspector*), Eddy Waller (*proprietor*), David Hughes (*Frank*), Cliff Clark (*townsman*), Adrian Morris (*agent*), Robert Homans (*Spencer*), Irving Bacon (*conductor*), Kitty McHugh (*Mae*).

The social indignation of John Steinbeck's novel *The Grapes of Wrath* was certainly the finest statement of faith in the common man published in the Thirties. Darryl F. Zanuck's decision to film the book indicated his business acumen and his ability to assess public taste. His courage, vision and careful choice of talents ensured that Steinbeck's work was brought to the screen virtually intact.

Nunnally Johnson's script (doctored by Zanuck) developed the central incidents of the book into a continuous pattern of action and narrative. Though it failed to chart fully the economic, political and social background, the script gained in power and simplicity what it lost in perspective. Johnson retained many lines of dialogue from the novel, but did not hesitate to switch them between characters

when it suited the dramatic purposes of the film; he avoided too many long monologues and invested the dialogue with the ring of the people's voice. The script was contractually bound to retain the theme of the book, and Steinbeck passed the script on August 8, 1939. Contrary to popular belief, Henry Fonda was not announced as the star until some time later.

Gregg Toland shot the bulk of the film using only natural light; his unhesitating use of darkness (at a time when most Hollywood films were brightly lit) enhances the picture's emotional power far more than Alfred Newman's unremarkable musical score. Toland's use of long shots punctuates the gruelling journey, both separating its incidents and linking them. His camera plays a more dynamic role in dramatic scenes.

Under John Ford's economical direction the film maintains its impetus until the end; and his knack of placing just the right face in the smallest role dignifies the supporting parts.

Fonda gives a fine, unsentimental performance as Tom Joad, often concealing his emotions beneath a mask of apologetic gruffness. After the death of Casy (John Carradine) – who embodies the

religious and political issues of the film – Tom inherits the former preacher's sense of mission; he renounces his personal identity to gain the larger one of 'leader of the people'. In contrast, the casting of Jane Darwell as his indomitable mother was a mistake. Though she won an Oscar for Best Supporting Actress, her plump niceness is plainly at odds with the lean, stringy, rawhide woman of the

4

novel. Ma Joad would have been superbly characterized by Beulah Bondi, who was the original choice for the part.

As the child of Irish parents, Ford was particularly attracted to the project since its story bore a resemblance to a similar situation that arose during the Irish famines of the 1840s; however, his vision became one of American pioneers opening up the West in search of a Garden of Eden. Yet his film breaks new ground by representing in human terms some of the grim costs and results of this pioneering drive. It touches on a few of the effects of land speculation and agricultural mechanization, dramatizing the plight of these victims of American history, and it achieves a more poignant impact than contemporary films like *Our Daily Bread* (1934), *The Trail of the Lonesome Pine* (1936) and *Of Human Hearts* (1938).

Documentaries, such as *The Plow That Broke the Plains* (1936) and *The River* (1938), and books, like *An American Exodus* and *Let Us Now Praise Famous Men*, had highlighted the image of the gaunt, hungry 'tractored-out' farmer, no longer menaced by Indians in his struggle to survive, but by the pitiless spectre of starvation. This was caused by wholesale evictions from farms by landowners who wished to employ new agricultural machinery. It cannot be said that *The Grapes of Wrath* fully faces up to this serious social issue; for example, the film eliminates the novel's description of the still-birth of Rosaharn's baby, which in context becomes a shocking indictment of society. In addition, the film's depiction of Tom Joad's conversion to the cause of working people is tainted with sentimentality.

At the film's premiere, the first three rows were reserved for officers and directors of the Chase National Bank and their wives. Ironically this was one of the institutions which controlled the western land companies that 'tractored' the Joads, and thousands like them, off their farms. The Bank was about to make further profits from this dramatization of their ex-tenants' plight, since they were also the bankers for the film's production company.   KINGSLEY CANHAM

Returning from a four-year prison sentence for killing a man, Tom Joad finds his Kansas home deserted. His family have been evicted by the land company who wish to farm the dying soil more economically using new agricultural machinery. Tom locates his family at the home of a relative.

They set out for California in a rickety old truck (1), but the 'promised land' soon dashes their hopes (2).

Lured to a miserable township by promises of work as fruit-pickers, they are hounded and exploited by unscrupulous farmers and labour agents and persecuted by townsfolk and corrupt state police (3). The family's moral strength is tested by death and separation (4). Casy, an unfrocked preacher, attempts to organize a strike for better conditions (5) and is murdered by strike-breakers. Tom revenges his death, but becomes a fugitive from justice, finding only temporary refuge at a government transit camp that is humanely run (6). He tells Ma Joad of his decision to carry on Casy's mission – to fight for the common rights of the working man (7). He leaves his mother determined to hold the remainder of the family together.

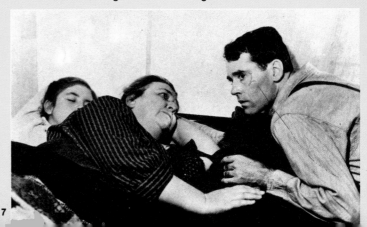

Directed by Orson Welles, 1940
Prod co: Mercury Productions/RKO. **exec prod:** George J. Schaefer. **prod:** Orson Welles. **sc:** Herman J. Mankiewicz, Orson Welles. **photo:** Gregg Toland. **sp eff:** Vernon L. Walker. **ed:** Robert Wise, Mark Robson. **art dir:** Van Nest Polglase, Darrell Silvera, Hilyard Brown. **cost:** Edward Stevenson. **mus:** Bernard Herrmann. **sd:** Bailey Fesler, James G. Stewart. **ass dir:** Richard Wilson. **r/t:** 119 minutes. New York premiere, 1 May 1941.
Cast: Orson Welles (*Charles Foster Kane*), Joseph Cotten (*Jedediah Leland*), Dorothy Comingore (*Susan Alexander*), Everett Sloane (*Mr Bernstein*), Ray Collins (*James W. Gettys*), George Coulouris (*Walter Parks Thatcher*), Agnes Moorehead (*Kane's mother*), Paul Stewart (*Raymond*), Ruth Warrick (*Emily Norton*), Erskine Sandford (*Herbert Carter*), William Alland (*Thompson; newsreel reader*), Fortunio Bonanova (*Matisti*), Gus Schilling (*head waiter*), Philip Van Zandt (*Mr Rawlston*), Georgia Backus (*Miss Anderson*), Harry Shannon (*Kane's father*), Sonny Bupp (*Kane III*), Buddy Swan (*Kane age 8*), Richard Barr (*Hillman*), Joan Blair (*Georgia*), Al Eben (*Mike*), Charles Bennett (*entertainer*), Milt Kibbee (*reporter*), Tom Curran (*Teddy Roosevelt*), Irving Mitchell (*Dr Corey*), Edith Evanson (*nurse*), Arthur Kay (*conductor*), Tudor Williams (*chorus master*), Herbert Corthell (*city editor*), Benny Rubin (*Smather*), Edmund Cobb (*reporter*), Frances Neal (*Ethel*), Robert Dudley (*photographer*), Ellen Lowe (*Miss Townsend*), Gino Corrado (*Gino the waiter*), Alan Ladd, Louise Currie, Eddie Coke, Walter Sande, Arthur O'Connell (*reporters*).

Charles Foster Kane utters his final word, 'Rosebud', and dies on his massive, crumbling estate, Xanadu (1).

Newsreel journalists prepare a film showing Kane's rise and fall, but it lacks an angle. A reporter is sent to find out who Rosebud may be. He interviews Susan Alexander (2) (Kane's second wife), Bernstein (3) and Jed Leland (two old employees) and Kane's butler, Raymond. Through them the jigsaw of Kane's life is pieced together.

Five-year-old Kane has inherited an immense fortune; at his mother's wish he is placed under the guardianship of banker Walter Thatcher (4) and is taken away from his Colorado home.

Thirty years later Kane buys up the New York *Inquirer* and begins his career as a scandal-sheet publisher (5). He marries Emily Norton (6) but later meets Susan Alexander (7) and establishes a love-nest with her. His attempt to run for governor (8) is shattered along with his marriage when political enemy Jim Gettys (9) exposes the affair.

Kane marries Susan and launches her on a disastrous career as an opera singer. But her failure and the set-backs he suffers during the Depression force him to retreat to his castle, Xanadu (10).

Susan, bored by the isolation of Xanadu and by Kane's autocratic behaviour, eventually leaves him. Kane dies and his chattels are disposed of, among them a childhood sled bearing the painted-on name of Rosebud (11).

1

4

2

3

7

8

9

Up to the Forties, orthodox Hollywood camera style consisted of diffused lighting and soft focus, even for such brutally realistic films as *I Am a Fugitive From a Chain Gang* (1932). Photographed in this way a typical sequence might consist of a long or medium establishing shot with cuts to close-up shots to show detail. Orson Welles' *Citizen Kane* (1940), however, signalled the beginning of a new period in American cinema. Composition in depth, obtained by increased depth-of-field photography, meant that images on several planes could all be held in sharp focus. The dramatic effects of a scene were created by images within the composition itself rather than by editing; and because both foreground and background remained in focus, the spectator could see everything there was to see in a single shot.

Depth of field in *Citizen Kane* results from a number of factors including the use of faster film and wide-angle lenses. These lenses possess certain inherent optical properties which can dramatically affect the appearance of a composition. As well as keeping foreground and background in focus, they create the illusion of perspective by exaggerating the relative scale of objects on different planes – objects closer to the camera appear much larger than those further away.

The relationship between visual style and narrative content seems almost inseparable in the film. The character of Kane is revealed not so much by what he says and does as by how he is made to appear in the context of his surroundings.

Early in the film there is a scene where Walter Thatcher has come to Colorado to take the young Kane away with him. In one of the shots (picture 4) Mrs Kane sits reading the terms of her son's inheritance in the foreground and at the right of the frame. Thatcher is seated slightly behind and to the right of her, and Kane's father stands at the left of the frame in the middle distance. By their position and size the three figures appear to be visually and dramatically at the centre of the scene. Initially their relative sizes on the screen seem to indicate their relative narrative importance: Mrs Kane, the mother who is trying to do the best for her son, is the dominant personality; Thatcher is the interloper; and the elder Kane, ineffectively voicing his opposition, is a figure of weakness. After looking through the foreground diagonally to the middle distance, attention centres on a window at the very back of the room. Through it can barely be identified the figure of a young boy who is all but obliterated by falling snow.

The boy may at first appear to be the least important figure in the composition, but the opposite is true. Much greater dramatic coherence is given to the scene when it is scanned in reverse order, from background to foreground. The smallest figure becomes the focal point of the narrative – it is Kane's future his parents and Thatcher are discussing, *his* life that, from that point onwards, will be irrevocably changed.

Time and again in the film secondary figures are positioned to act as a frame within the film frame in order to concentrate the spectator's attention on Kane in the distance. But a point occurs during the political rally sequence where, although a similar framing technique is used, the dramatic effect is suddenly reversed. Kane is giving the supreme performance of his career: his magnificent rhetoric about protecting working men, slum children and ordinary citizens alike captivates the audience. The scene ends, however, with a shot (picture 9) that dispels this effect and signals the beginning of the end for Kane. Political boss Jim Gettys is seen standing high up in a balcony, his figure filling the right side of the frame. To the left and far below, Kane is finishing his speech to wild applause. But the exaggerated perspective and the disproportionate size of Gettys foreshadows the despairing events about to befall Kane.

Up to this point in the film Kane is depicted as being in control of space on the screen. The spectator's attention, manipulated by the expressive dynamics of the composition and lighting, is unerringly drawn to him. But from the time he loses the election to the end of the film, his presence is made to seem increasingly insignificant in relation to his surroundings. This is most noticeable in the concluding scenes of Kane and Susan's self-imposed exile in Xanadu where Kane appears dwarfed by the volume of the rooms and the sheer depth of the huge, gaping fireplace. Space in the cavernous mausoleum of Xanadu now controls Kane and isolates him in a void of darkness.

ARNOLD DESSER

5

6

10

11

1

Ivan the Terrible

Eisenstein's project to make a film about Tsar Ivan IV – *Ivan the Terrible* – was accepted for production at Mosfilm in 1941 but inevitably delayed by the German invasion of the USSR which began in June of that year. When filming finally started in 1943, Moscow was still under attack, so the film was shot at the Alma Ata studios in the heart of Central Asia.

The scenario was conceived in two parts, but in production Eisenstein extended the piece to become a trilogy, a decision which was to cause the authorities to misunderstand the nature of the film and view a part of it with grave disapproval.

Ivan IV was the ruler who in the sixteenth century completed the task (begun by his grandfather Ivan III) of uniting the Russian lands under a single autocrat or Tsar. In the process he overcame rival feudal princes, drove out the Tartars and paved the way for an opening for the province of Rus upon the Baltic Sea – finally achieved 150 years later by Peter the Great.

As with his previous film, *Alexander Nevsky* (1938), Eisenstein certainly intended *Ivan the Terrible* to arouse patriotic pride in Russia's past achievements and heroes as part of the preparation for the coming German onslaught. What especially interested him was the human aspect of this historical re-creation; he was fascinated by the personality of a man who combined constructive idealism with growing ruthlessness.

Was Ivan indeed 'Terrible' – a monster? Had he been so the project would have been far less interesting. Undoubtedly the struggle for national identity and royal absolutism led to the committing of vile deeds. But, as Eisenstein reminds us, the century that Ivan lived in was one of widespread bloody and bitter conflict throughout Europe. It is only in recent times that the word 'Terrible' has acquired its evil overtones in English. The Russian word applied to Ivan – *Grozny* – has much more the meaning of 'awe-inspiring'. It was this awe of majesty that Eisenstein sought to create throughout the film.

He adopted many special devices for this purpose. The acting is in an intense, almost ritualistic style, quite unlike the realistic use of natural settings, persons and movements for which he became famous in his early work. To em-phasize the complex duality of his subject he used two master cameramen, adding to the limpid clarity of Tissé's exteriors the glitter and darkness of Moskvin's interiors, so expressive of intrigue. He used colour in one reel, and in an unusual way, not to imitate nature but to heighten the drama. The composer Prokofiev and he married the rhythms of music and image more closely than ever before. He also used a new method of cutting away towards the end of a character's speech so that his closing lines were superimposed on the image of the listener – thus focusing attention on his reaction and redoubling the impact of the words.

The exact action as filmed can be studied in the script published beforehand. It is set out in a series of magnificent episodes: Ivan's assertion of authority against his regents while yet a boy; his self-coronation as Tsar in the Cathedral of the Assumption at the age of 17; his luxurious wedding, and the quelling, by his personal domination alone, of a panicky crowd; the defeat of Tartar might at the city of Kazan; the treachery of the boyars (nobles) and disloyalty of his friends when he lies ill; the poisoning of his consort by his foes; his withdrawal from Moscow and triumphant return to the city.

Here ends *Part One*. It reached the Soviet screen at the end of 1944, and two years later was awarded the Stalin Prize First Class for cinema for that year.

Part Two of the scenario depicts Ivan's terrible revenge. He draws closer around him his 'iron ring' of guards – the *oprichniki* or 'men apart' – to slaughter his enemies. He frustrates a plot by his kinsfolk to assassinate him in an amazing cathedral scene. Finally, despite corruption and treachery even within the ranks of his own 'Tsar's men', he eventually leads his troops against the Teutonic castles to reach the Baltic shore.

Inevitably, by dividing the intended second part, and separating off its beginning of claustrophobic horror as *Tale Two: The Boyars' Plot*, with the end, the attainment of the goal of unification, to come in yet a third, Eisenstein obscured, so far as practical viewing was concerned, the balance of the whole.

Tale Two was ready in 1946. In the circumstances it was not altogether surprising that, when the Central Committee of the Soviet Communist Party decided to take several famous directors to task, they sharply criticized this film for untruth. Ivan, they said, had become Hamlet-like, 'a man of no will and little character,' and his guards 'Klu Klux Klan-like degenerates'. It is ironical that *Pravda* published this criticism just as Eisenstein and his friends were celebrating the award for *Part One*. Purely coincidentally, without yet knowing of this, he collapsed with a heart attack while dancing at the festivities. He recovered slowly in the VIP's hospital, and it was agreed that when well enough he should work on completing *Ivan the Terrible* as a two-part film using sequences from *Tale Two*, reels already made for 'Three' – four of which are said to have been finished but have disappeared – and shooting final scenes on the Baltic shore. But his convalescence was slow; he wrote and lectured a little, then died from a second attack in 1948 while writing an article on the film's use of colour.

The ban on *Tale Two* was lifted only in 1958, after 12 years' waiting, and immediately had an overwhelming success at the International Fair in Brussels, completing the extraordinary, though unfinished, legacy of this remarkable director.

IVOR MONTAGU

2

3

4

5

6

1 The coronation of Ivan, the young Grand Duke of Muscovy, as Tsar of Rus.

2 The royal wedding feast of Ivan and his bride Anastasia.

3 Ivan at the siege of Kazan, at which he defeats the Tartars.

4 Ivan swears vengeance on the coffin of his wife, poisoned by the nobles.

5 Ivan secludes himself in a monastery, but the people of Moscow beg him to return and rule over them.

6 The Tsar's aunt plots to kill Ivan and place her son, Vladimir, on the throne in his stead.

7 At a banquet, Vladimir, fuddled, incautiously reveals his aunt's plot.

8 Apparently in high spirits, Ivan calls for the royal regalia and persuades Vladimir to head the procession to evening prayer clad in the royal robes.

9 The assassin, hired by the aunt to kill Ivan, strikes her own son by mistake.

Directed by Sergei Eisenstein. Part One, 1944; Part Two (Tale Two: The Boyars' Plot), 1946

Prod co: Mosfilm. **sc:** Sergei Eisenstein. **photo:** Andrei Moskvin, Edouard Tissé. **art dir:** Isaak Shpinel. **mus:** Sergei Prokofiev. **lyr:** V. Lugovsky. **ass dir:** B. Sveshnikov, L. Indenblom. Moscow premiere of Part One, 30 December 1944.

Cast: Nikolai Cherkasov (*Ivan*), Ludmila Tselikovskaya (*Anastasia Romanovna, the Tsaritsa*), Mikhail Zharov (*Malyuta Skuratov*), A. Buma (*Alexei Basmanov*), M. Kuznetsov (*Fyodor, Basmanov's son*), Serafina Birman (*Euphrosyne Staritsky, the Tsar's aunt*), Pavel Kadochnikov (*Vladimir Staritsky, her son*), Mikhail Nazvanov (*Prince Andrew Kurbsky*), Andrei Abrikosov (*Boyar Fyodor Kolychev, later Metropolitan Philip*), Alexander Mgebrov (*Pimen, Archbishop of Novgorod*), V.I. Pudovkin (*a beggar fanatic*), A. Balashov (*Peter Volynets*), Pavel Massalsky, (*King Sigismund of Poland*), Eric Pyriev (*Ivan as a boy*).

8

9

UN FILM DE
MARCEL CARNÉ

ARLETTY · JEAN-LOUIS BARRAULT · PIERRE BRASSEUR · PIERRE RENOIR

LES ENFANTS DU PARADIS

avec LOUIS SALOU MARCEL HERRAND et MARIA CASARÈS

IMAGES DE ROGER HUBERT
DIRECTEUR DE PRODUCTION FRED ORAIN

SCÉNARIO ET DIALOGUES DE JACQUES PRÉVERT

Directed by Marcel Carné, 1945
Prod co: Pathé-Cinéma. **prod:** Fred Orain. **prod man:** Raymond Borderie. **sc:** Jacques Prévert. **photo:** Roger Hubert. **ed:** Henri Rust. **art dir:** Léon Barsacq, R. Gabutti, Alexandre Trauner. **mus:** Joseph Kosma, Maurice Thiriet, G. Mouqué. **cost:** Mayo. **r/t:** 195 minutes. Paris premiere, 9 March 1945. Released in the USA as *Children of Paradise*.
Cast: Arletty (*Garance*), Jean-Louis Barrault (*Baptiste Debureau*), Pierre Brasseur (*Frédéric Lemaître*), Maria Casarès (*Nathalie*), Marcel Herrand (*Lacenaire*), Louis Salou (*Count Edouard de Montray*), Pierre Renoir (*Jéricho*), Paul Frankeur (*inspector*), Jane Marken (*Mme Hermine*), Fabien Loris (*Avril*), Etienne Decroux (*Anselme Debureau*), Marcel Pérès (*director of the Funambules*), Gaston Modot (*File de Soie, the blind man*), Pierre Palau (*manager of the Funambules*), Jacques Castelot (*Georges*), Robert Dhéry (*Celestin*), Rognoni (*director of the Grand Theatre*), Florencie (*gendarme*), Guy Favières (*cashier*), Albert Remy (*Scarpia Borigni*), Auguste Bovério (*first author*), Paul Demange (*second author*), Jean Diener (*third author*), Habib Benglia (*boy from Turkish baths*).

Marcel Carné once said that *Les Enfants du Paradis* (*Children of Paradise*) was a tribute to the theatre, and indeed the film is an evocation of the stage in the days when it still belonged to the people and before it became the haunt of the fashionable upper classes. 'Paradis', in fact, is what in English we should call 'the gods' – the heights sacred to the public sitting in the gallery. And 'the children' are both the actors – beloved (or not) by that audience watching from those heavenly heights – and the audience themselves. The close relationship between public and performer has gone now. It lingered with the music-hall, but the music-hall itself has dwindled and vanished. Perhaps the remembrance of it has helped to give Carné's piece its enormous success.

The idea for the film, it seems, belonged to the actor Jean-Louis Barrault. The second year of the Occupation saw Marcel Carné and his screenwriter, the poet Jacques Prévert, ready to begin making a new film. Working together they had enjoyed great prestige both before the war and during it; but now one of their projects had run into difficulties and they needed a fresh subject. Barrault, whom they encountered in a café in Nice, suggested a film about Baptiste Debureau, the Funambules and the Boulevard du Crime. Debureau had been the most celebrated of French mimes; the Funambules, in the Boulevard du Temple, was the theatre where he performed; the Boulevard du Temple was sometimes called the Boulevard du Crime because it was notorious for murders. Violence, the romance of the popular theatre, and a famous historical figure – everybody agreed that the possibilities were seductive, and work began on the script which, though fictional, was to be based on real-life characters – not only Debureau, but also the stage actor Frédéric Lemaître and the dandy and notorious criminal Lacenaire.

It was a work of happy cooperation. Carné and Prévert, of course, were the chief creators; the designer Alexandre Trauner assisted, as did Joseph Kosma the composer; while the actors, Barrault (Debureau), Pierre Brasseur (Lemaître) and Marcel Herrand (Lacenaire) joined in to discuss their roles. After six months preparation, Carné began shooting.

An authentic setting had to be provided to establish the relation-

1

2

ship between the two actors and their public and to revive the mood and the popular feeling of mid-nineteenth-century Paris. This posed formidable problems; because of the war, materials were scarce – indeed, everything was scarce. Yet somehow a section of the Boulevard du Temple, theatre-fronts and all, was reconstructed – stretching for a quarter of a mile. Carné employed 25,000 extras to act as the carnival crowd, with its entertainers, jugglers, tight-rope walkers and weight-lifters, and the yelling audience of the Funambules theatre.

Les Enfants du Paradis took three years to complete, and at the time was probably the most expensive film ever to be made in France. Certainly it was the grandest of Carné's films; he was never to make another as masterly. It was not a work noted for discovering new talents. Most of the players – Pierre Brasseur, Pierre Renoir, the lovely Arletty – were already established. Barrault, although he made occasional and powerful appearances on the screen, was essentially a stage actor. Only Maria Casarès went on to greater fame, playing the role of Death in Jean Cocteau's *Orphée* (1950).

The film itself, however, was a lasting triumph. For the French, just emerging from years of Occupation, the romantic brilliance of *Les Enfants du Paradis* was a testimony to survival and a reassertion of French elegance and artistry. As Carné said, it was a tribute to the theatre – a French theatre with French performers. It may also be said to have been a declaration of the resilience of France herself.

DILYS POWELL

The story of Garance, a beautiful, independent girl, and the four men who love her unfolds against a background of the popular theatre and the underworld of Paris in the 1840s (1). The girl is saved from arrest for theft by Baptiste, a mime artist, who explains in gestures that she is not guilty; the thief was her criminal companion Lacenaire. Baptiste finds her work in the theatre (2) and shelters her, but out of delicacy refrains from taking advantage of her willingness to love. She becomes the mistress of his friend, the would-be actor Frédéric; later, to save herself from a police charge (3), she accepts the protection of the Count, a rich aristocrat (4), and leaves Paris.

When she returns, Frédéric and Baptiste, now married to Nathalie, a girl from the theatre (5), are both famous. Five years have passed, but Garance and Baptiste are still in love. They are reunited (6) but betrayed by Lacenaire, who in his vicious fashion also loves Garance. He is insulted by the Count (7) and murders him (8). Nathalie discovers the lovers and her pitiful pleas drive Garance to disappear, leaving Baptiste vainly pursuing her through the crowded boulevard.

3

4

5

6

7

8

27

Noel Coward's
BRIEF ENCOUNTER
starring
CELIA JOHNSON · TREVOR HOWARD
with
STANLEY HOLLOWAY
JOYCE CAREY · CYRIL RAYMOND

Brief Encounter was not particularly successful at the box-office following its release in November 1945, although, as David Lean wrote in 1947, 'The film did very well in what are known as the better-class halls'. One critic thought it was 'more like a French film', which at the time was the highest of praise. Indeed, *Brief Encounter* won the main prize at the first Cannes Film Festival.

Lean attributed its relative commercial failure to its lack of star names. He wrote in *Penguin Film Review No. 4*: 'There was an unhappy ending. The film was played out in unglamorous surroundings. And the three leading characters were approaching middle-age.'

An additional factor must have been the film's timing: with the euphoria and the traumas of the immediate post-war period, when people were picking up the threads of their lives, audiences could hardly be expected to enjoy seeing the drabness and frustrations of life reflected on the screen, no matter how sensitively portrayed. At the same time, the picture of pre-war Home Counties life that the film conjured up may well have seemed like a foreign land to audiences in 1945; seen today, it is a dream of England long ago.

Lean's fascinating essay on *Brief Encounter* highlights what many critics regard as the film's chief virtue: its honest depiction of ordinary folk unable to cope with emotions outside their experience. Rather than surrender to their instincts, Laura and Alec abandon their unconsummated affair out of a sense of shame. The middle-class code, built around loyalty to hearth and home, remains intact.

Richard Winnington's *News Chronicle* review neatly summarizes contemporary attitudes to the film which have been perpetuated ever since. 'Polished as is this film,' he wrote, 'its strength does not lie in movie technique, of which there is plenty, so much as in the tight realism of its detail.' This is a subtle way of acclaiming Noel Coward's one-act play *Still Life*, on which *Brief Encounter* was based, at the expense of Lean's cinematic dexterity. Yet what is striking about the film is not its realism but how Lean manipulates a realist framework to create a haunting fantasy. While the principal settings are realistic (the smokey station buffet; the Kardomah restaurant, complete with ladies' orchestra; Laura's modest semi-detached house), the narrative structure is certainly not. Laura and Alec's country outings, where they discover (or re-discover) sexual desire, are pantheist visions which will be a preoccupation of Lean's later work. And beside the dimly-lit interiors and the invigorating country scenery are the images of *film noir* – the rain-washed streets, the litter-strewn subway where Laura and Alec steal a furtive kiss, the sense of being trapped within a repressive social system.

The film is a memory, or reverie; as Laura begins to recall her affair, Lean superimposes a shot of her sitting by the hearth on the first image of the flashback. Laura's visit to the cinema with Alec, where they watch a trailer for 'Flames of Passion', based on the novel 'Gentle Summer', articulates the element of fantasy within the film. Time-honoured romantic imagery is also powerfully present when, on the train, Laura has visions of herself dancing at a ball, being romanced in a gondola and watching the sun go down in the South Seas. When Laura's husband asks her help with a Keats quotation in *The Times* crossword, she is able to answer immediately, 'Romance'. 'That's right,' says her husband, 'it

Directed by David Lean, 1945
Prod co: Independent Producers/Cineguild. **prod:** Noel Coward. **assoc prod:** Ronald Neame, Anthony Havelock-Allan. **sc:** David Lean, Ronald Neame, Anthony Havelock-Allan, Noel Coward, from the play *Still Life* by Noel Coward. **photo:** Robert Krasker, B. Francke. **ed:** Jack Harris, Harry Miller. **art dir:** L. P. Williams, G. E. Calthrop. **mus:** Rachmaninov's Second Piano Concerto played by Eileen Joyce and the National Symphony Orchestra conducted by Muir Matheson. **sd:** Stanley Lambourne, Desmond Dew. **ass dir:** George Pollock. **prod man:** E. Holding. **r/t:** 86 minutes. London premiere, 26 November 1945.
Cast: Celia Johnson (*Laura Jesson*), Trevor Howard (*Dr Alec Harvey*), Cyril Raymond (*Fred Jesson*), Stanley Holloway (*Albert Godby, station guard*), Joyce Carey (*Myrtle Bagot*), Margaret Barton (*Beryl Waters*), Valentine Dyall (*Stephen Lynn*), Beverly Gregg (*Dolly Messiter*), Nuna Davey (*Mrs Rolandson*), George V. Sheldon (*clergyman*), Jack May (*boatman*), Edward Hodge (*Bill*), Wilfred Babbage (*policeman*), Henrietta Vincent (*Margaret*), Dennis Harkin (*Stanley*), Marjorie Mars (*Mary Norton*), Irene Handl (*organist*), Sydney Bromley (*Johnnie*), Avis Scutt (*waitress*), Richard Thomas (*Bobbie*), Wally Bosco (*doctor*).

4

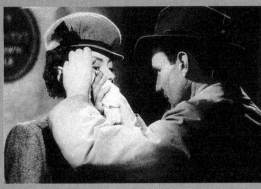

5

7

8

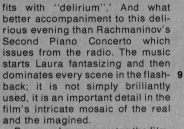

9

10

fits with "delirium." And what better accompaniment to this delirious evening than Rachmaninov's Second Piano Concerto which issues from the radio. The music starts Laura fantasizing and then dominates every scene in the flashback; it is not simply brilliantly used, it is an important detail in the film's intricate mosaic of the real and the imagined.

Because Laura narrates the film, we must beware of taking everything at face value – the characters are subjective reflections of her sense of romanticism and her sense of guilt. So Alec is without flaws, handsome, considerate, intelligent and a doctor dedicated to saving children's lives, while Laura's husband is dependable, loving yet shown to be helpless when their child is taken ill; he needs the love and support of his wife. Similarly, the much-criticized portrayals of the always-on-duty station guard (Stanley Holloway) and the buffet waitress who affects an upper-class accent (Joyce Carey) are deliberate caricatures; their openly sexual banter is in ironic contrast to Laura and Alec's repressed passion (superbly conveyed by the performances of Celia Johnson and Trevor Howard in his first starring role).

Brief Encounter remains a remarkably complex film, and if aspects of it have passed into the mythology and cliché of the British cinema, there is more than enough left to fascinate and move us still.
ADRIAN TURNER

11

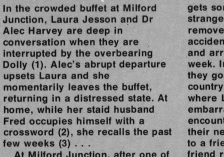

12

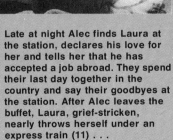

In the crowded buffet at Milford Junction, Laura Jesson and Dr Alec Harvey are deep in conversation when they are interrupted by the overbearing Dolly (1). Alec's abrupt departure upsets Laura and she momentarily leaves the buffet, returning in a distressed state. At home, while her staid husband Fred occupies himself with a crossword (2), she recalls the past few weeks (3) . . .

At Milford Junction, after one of her weekly shopping trips, Laura gets some grit in her eye which a stranger, Alec, delicately removes (4). They meet again by accident (5), go to the cinema (6) and arrange to meet the following week. In the succeeding weeks, they go to the park (7), to the country (8) and to a restaurant, where Laura is mortified with embarrassment when she encounters some old friends. At their next meeting, Alec takes her to a friend's flat but when the friend returns unexpectedly (9), Laura runs away ashamed (10).

Late at night Alec finds Laura at the station, declares his love for her and tells her that he has accepted a job abroad. They spend their last day together in the country and say their goodbyes at the station. After Alec leaves the buffet, Laura, grief-stricken, nearly throws herself under an express train (11) . . .

She emerges from her reverie to find Fred kneeling by her side (12). 'You've been a long way away,' he says gently, 'Thank you for coming back to me.'

Sunset Boulevard is a 20-mile stretch of asphalt which begins a few blocks from the Dorothy Chandler Pavilion, venue for the Academy Awards presentations, then proceeds with scant ceremony through Downtown Los Angeles. It straightens out for the tawdry Strip and then winds its way gracefully past the pools and green-baize lawns of Beverly Hills, Bel Air and Brentwood before its progress is dramatically halted by the Ocean.

Socially and topographically Sunset Boulevard has many identities, but emotionally it evokes only one thing: Hollywood. How appropriate, then, that Billy Wilder's film, so attuned to Hollywood's bloodstream, should take its title from this principal artery.

Ironically, the mansion used in the film was not on Sunset Boulevard at all. It belonged to the Getty family (who demolished it in 1957) and the address was 3810 Wilshire Boulevard. Wilder and his team of Paramount designers obtained permission to use the mansion on condition they installed a swimming pool, which became the film's metaphor for success – much coveted by the hero – and its symbol of decay. When we first glimpse the pool it is empty and there are rats scuttling on the rubbish-strewn floor. During the course of the film the pool is restored and at the end it receives the bullet-riddled corpse of the hero.

It is the hero, Joe Gillis (William Holden), who narrates the film and it is only at the end that the spectator realizes he is dead. His is literally a voice from the grave, giving additional irony to his role as a writer for Norma Desmond (Gloria Swanson), a long-forgotten silent star whose delusions of continuing fame bring about Joe's murder. This unusual narrative device, delivered by Joe in tones evocative of B pictures and imitation Scott Fitzgerald, draws attention to Sunset Boulevard as an anthology of Hollywood style.

The Miss Havisham-like mansion, with wheezing organ, oppressive decor and accumulation of bric-a-brac from the past, plus a mysterious butler and even a midnight burial for a pet monkey, links Sunset Boulevard to the horror genre. The opening car chase recalls the gangster films of the Thirties. Norma's impersonations of Chaplin and Mack Sennett bathing beauties place silent slapstick in a disturbing context. The backlot

A HOLLYWOOD STORY
Sensational...
Daring...
Unforgettable!

SUNSET BOULEVARD

WILLIAM HOLDEN · GLORIA SWANSON · ERICH von STROHEIM

NANCY OLSON · FRED CLARK · LLOYD GOUGH · JACK WEBB
CECIL B. DeMILLE · HEDDA HOPPER · BUSTER KEATON · ANNA Q. NILSSON · H.B. WARNER · FRANKLYN FARNUM

romance between Joe and Betty resembles the star-struck Paramount comedies of Mitchell Leisen and Preston Sturges – contaminated, though, by Joe's double life with Norma. Wilder's bravura mise-en-scène, the macabre atmosphere, the assertive females and suppliant males finally locate Sunset Boulevard at the intersection of film noir and Gothic melodrama.

The casting (with which Wilder had problems – Mae West and Pola Negri turned him down and Montgomery Clift backed out at the last minute) takes his allusiveness several stages further. Consider the sequence in which Norma shows Joe one of her old films. This is no mock-up. It is the legendary and unfinished Queen Kelly (1928), starring Gloria Swanson and directed by Erich von Stroheim who, in Sunset Boulevard, plays Norma's butler, ex-husband and ex-director. It is a bizarre scene as Stroheim shows his own work, his star transfixed by the youthful images of herself, crying 'I'll show them! I'll be back up there, so help me!' as her Medusa-like head is momentarily caught in the beam of the projector. And sitting calmly beside her is the

young would-be screenwriter, unmoved and contemptuous of the silent images.

Cecil B. DeMille appears as himself, seen at work on Samson and Delilah and greeting Norma as he used to greet Gloria Swanson at the same studio in the Twenties. There are 'The Waxworks', as Joe calls them – Buster Keaton, Anna Q. Nilsson and H.B. Warner, who play bridge at the mansion. And there is the notorious gossip columnist Hedda Hooper, appearing as herself but apparently not realizing that Wilder was portraying her as a vulture.

These Pirandellian effects are the source of the film's enduring power and fascination. As we watch actors playing roles in which they watch themselves playing roles, our ability to distinguish between illusion and reality is as severely tested as Norma's, except that we have Joe to guide us through the labyrinth while Norma is engulfed by the dream she has clung to so desperately.

If Wilder creates a vivid sense of the past, he also creates a vivid sense of the present. The four main characters – Norma and Max, Joe and Betty – represent a collision between the old and the new Hollywood, the former associated with grandeur, the latter with meanness. There is a great deal of wit, but never at Norma's expense. 'You know, pictures have changed quite a bit', says DeMille with barely concealed regret, and the film's most famous dialogue exchange demonstrates perfectly where its writers' sympathies lie: 'You're Norma Desmond. You used to be in silent pictures. You used to be big', says Joe. 'I am big' replies Norma, her eyes flaring, 'It's the pictures that got small.'

ADRIAN TURNER

7

11

A body is found floating in the swimming pool (1) at the mansion owned by Norma Desmond, a forgotten silent star, on Sunset Boulevard. Joe Gillis, a failed screenwriter (2), recalls the events leading up to this murder.

He is pursued by creditors who want to confiscate his car (3) and takes refuge in Norma's decrepit home (4–5) where she lives with her butler Max, formerly her husband and director (6). Joe accepts Norma's invitation to help write her screenplay of Salome (7),

Directed by Billy Wilder, 1950
Prod co: Paramount. **prod:** Charles Brackett. **sc:** Charles Brackett, D.M. Marshman Jr, Billy Wilder. **photo:** John F. Seitz, Farciot Edouart. **sp eff:** Gordon Jennings. **ed sup:** Doane Harrison. **ed:** Arthur Schmidt. **art dir:** Hans Dreier, John Meehan, Sam Comer, Ray Moyer. **mus:** Franz Waxman, 'Salome's Dance of the Veils' by Richard Strauss. **sd:** John Cope, Harry Lindgren. **ass dir:** C.C. Coleman Jr. **r/t:** 111 minutes. New York premiere, 10 August 1950.
Cast: Gloria Swanson (Norma Desmond), William Holden (Joe Gillis), Erich von Stroheim (Max von Mayerling), Nancy Olson (Betty Shaefer), Fred Clark (Sheldrake), Jack Webb (Artie Green), Lloyd Gough (Morino), Buster Keaton, Anna Q. Nilsson, H.B. Warner ('The Waxworks'), Cecil B. DeMille, Hedda Hopper, Ray Evans, Jay Livingston (themselves), Franklyn Farnum (undertaker), Larry Blake, Charles Dayton (finance men).

1

SUNSET BLVD.

4

5

8

9

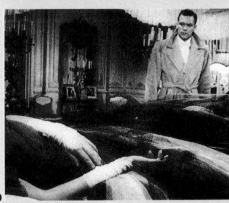

12

13

with which she plans a comeback, and soon he becomes her pet, accepting gifts of clothing and jewellery.

After a few weeks Joe, bored by Norma's film shows and dreams of the past (8), slips out to a party where he meets Betty (9), a reader at Paramount. When Norma attempts to commit suicide (10), Joe finds himself unable to desert her. Joe and Betty work together on an original screenplay and fall in love. Norma visits the studio and hopes that Cecil B. DeMille will direct her next picture (11). She finds out about Betty and Joe decides to extricate himself.

At the mansion he reveals to Betty his squalid existence with Norma and, later, when he tries to leave (12), he is shot dead by Norma, his body landing in the swimming pool (13). The police and reporters arrive and Norma, now completely mad, is lured downstairs by the news cameras (14–15), believing herself to be making *Salome* at last.

15

A DELUGE OF *Delight*—
SPLASHED WITH SONG HITS!

METRO-GOLDWYN-MAYER *presents*

Singin' in the Rain

IN COLOUR BY
TECHNICOLOR ®

Starring

Gene KELLY ★ Donald O'CONNOR
Debbie REYNOLDS ★ Cyd CHARISSE

1

2 / **3**

If there is one image which sums up the MGM musical, it is this: Gene Kelly, walking home in euphoric mood, is caught in a particularly heavy fall of Californian dew. But does he care? No, not a bit of it. On along the empty street, past the glamorous shop windows he dances, twirling under a water spout, tap-dancing in the gutter, finally stamping around with child-like delight and abandon in a giant puddle which covers half the road. When a mystified and vaguely hostile policeman comes up to find out just what is going on, Kelly has a simple answer: 'Just singin', and dancin', in the rain.'

The convention of the musical as a never-never land, where normal rules of life were for the moment suspended and invisible orchestras would accompany ordinary people as they expressed their ordinary emotions in an extraordinary way, found its complete justification in the integrated musicals of producer Arthur Freed. *Singin' in the Rain* is the finest hour of this school of film-making. It does, it is true, contain elements of the old 'putting on a show' musical formula (or in this case a film), but hardly any of its numbers are tied down to a stuffily rational context. Even the ambitious 'Broadway Melody' sequence is presented as a fantasy in the minds of its creators which they are trying to put over to their reluctant boss – and which he stubbornly fails to visualize.

In *Singin' in the Rain*, as in all the best musicals, the characters' behaviour has its own logic: song and dance are kept in reserve for the moments of irrepressible high spirits, passionate romance and the like, those moments when we might all feel like bursting into song or whirling away into dance if only we knew how, if only we were not worried what passers-by might think, if only we had the MGM orchestra and chorus to hand.

The title number is the climax of the film, but it is also the simplest. At the other end of the scale is the big 'Broadway Melody' number, which

Above right: a publicity shot of the film's opening scene

tells a show-business rags-to-riches story in miniature with a multiplicity of sets, costumes and extras. As a sizzling addition to the proceedings, Cyd Charisse features as the hero's dream woman.

The film's story manages to comprehend both these extremes. The script by Betty Comden and Adolph Green (both of whom had already worked with directors Gene Kelly and Stanley Donen on their first great success, *On the Town*, 1949) is probably the funniest and sharpest ever invented for a film musical. The image that it offers of Hollywood at the coming of sound has the ring of truth, for all its comic exaggeration. Who can forget the picture of the nitwit silent-movie queen Lina Lamont wrestling with round vowels as she bleats 'I caaan't stan'm' in response to her voice coach's patient tuition? Or the opening sequence in which her opposite number, romantic idol Don Lockwood reminisces for the listening public about his rise to the top, with 'dignity, dignity, always dignity', while the scenes of dancing for pennies and tatty burlesque which flash before us belie every word he says? Or the unstoppable *élan* with which Don and his two fellow conspirators, once they hit on the perfect solution to their dilemma (make the disastrous costume movie into a musical), burst into 'Good Morning' and gyrate and tap all over Don's beautiful, baronial, Hollywood home?

However, it is invidious to pick out any single treasure in *Singin' in the Rain* without mentioning all the rest. None of its stars were ever shown to better advantage and the formidable MGM machine never worked more smoothly or to greater effect, down to the last detail of design and orchestration. Whatever happened to the Hollywood musical in later years, *Singin' in the Rain* survives as irrefutable testimony to the wonderful way they were. JOHN RUSSELL TAYLOR **10**

6 / **7**

10 / **11**

Directed by Gene Kelly and Stanley Donen, 1952
Prod co: MGM. **prod:** Arthur Freed. **sc:** Betty Comden, Adolph Green. **photo:** Harold Rosson. **col:** Technicolor. **ed:** Adrienne Fazan. **art dir:** Cedric Gibbons, Randall Duell. **mus dir:** Lennie Hayton. **mus:** Nacio Herb Brown. **lyr:** Arthur Freed. **r/t:** 103 minutes.
Cast: Gene Kelly (*Don Lockwood*), Donald O'Connor (*Cosmo Brown*), Debbie Reynolds (*Kathy Selden*), Jean Hagen (*Lina Lamont*), Millard Mitchell (*R. F. Simpson*), Rita Moreno (*Zelda Zanders*), Douglas Fowley (*Roscoe Dexter*), Madge Blake (*Dora Bailey*), King Donovan (*Rod*), Kathleen Freeman (*Phoebe Dinsmore*), Bobby Watson (*diction coach*), Tommy Farrell (*Sid Phillips*).

Hollywood, 1927. Don Lockwood and Lina Lamont, famous stars of the silent screen, arrive at the premiere of their latest romantic swashbuckler (1). Don entertains the radio public with a conveniently laundered account of his rise from vaudeville (2) to stardom opposite Lina. On his way to a party after the film, Don is mobbed by fans and seeks refuge in the car of an aspiring actress, Kathy Selden (3). She piques Don by making 'superior' remarks about the movie business.

At the party, where Don's producer, R. F. Simpson, demonstrates talking pictures (4), a huge cake is brought in. Out of it pops none other than Kathy herself. Don makes fun of her; she throws a pie at him, hitting Lina by mistake, and vanishes.

Don looks in vain for Kathy, but his friend, Cosmo Brown, cheers him up with a song about the entertainer's lot (5).

Following the tremendous success of *The Jazz Singer*, Simpson orders the instant conversion of Don and Lina's new film, *The Duelling Cavalier*, to sound. Don has no real trouble with this, but Lina's squeaky Brooklyn accent and inability to speak into the microphone drive the director to distraction (6). While making the movie, Don encounters Kathy, who has a bit part in a musical being made at the studio; he makes his peace with her and declares his love (7). On the way home, Don sings and dances with joy during a cloudburst (8).

The premiere of *The Duelling Cavalier* is a hilarious disaster. That night, Don, Kathy and Cosmo come up with the idea that matters can be retrieved if the film is quickly turned into a musical and Lina's voice replaced by Kathy's (9). Don and Cosmo tell Simpson their adventurous plans, which concern the story of a young dancer's success on Broadway (10) and his involvement with an exotic nightclub queen (11). Simpson does not share the boys' enthusiasm but agrees to make *The Duelling Cavalier* into a musical.

Lina discovers that her voice has been dubbed by Kathy, whom she jealously regards as the the breaker of her (non-existent) romance with Don. By a clause in her contract she seems able to confine Kathy to being for ever her voice in films. But when Lina decides to 'sing' following the triumphant premiere of the revamped movie, Don and Cosmo reveal to the audience that Lina's vocal talents really belong to Kathy. Kathy becomes a star in her own right, and she and Don live happily ever after (12).

4

5

8

9

12

The plot for the three films of *A Star Is Born* (1937, 1954 and 1976) is based upon two things: the acidic satire of film-land ethics that came from George Cukor's *What Price Hollywood?* (1932) and the watery suicide in 1935 of the silent star John Bowers. In their story of the rise of a talented young star and the plummeting career of her alcoholic husband and mentor, the films draw upon this material, neutralizing the bitterness and glamorizing the facts.

The 1937 non-musical version, directed by William Wellman, is nevertheless fast-paced and abrasive with a keen eye for locations. The 1976 film, directed by Frank Pierson, suffers from having nothing much to say about the already familiar plot, except an update to the world of rock music where drugs replace booze. The great success of the trio though, is undoubtedly Cukor's in 1954: a film whose rich emotional range and imaginative utilization of the showbiz milieu completely overshadows the other two films.

Judy Garland was peculiarly right for the role. It is impossible to watch this *A Star Is Born* without reflecting on the problems of Garland's own life. And this factor resulted in her most electrifying performance. By this stage in her career, no gesture or expression was wasted, and she turns the torchy interlude of a song like 'The Man That Got Away' into a small powerhouse of its own.

As flawed as it is by cuts and alien insertions which interfere with the director's original conception, it is still arguably one of Cukor's best pictures. It allowed him to explore his usual preoccupation with theatricality and role-playing as never before. A dramatic addition in this exploration was his use of colour (previously confined to one sequence in *The Women*, 1939) and CinemaScope. In this venture, Cukor was aided by the fashion photographer Hoyningen-Huene. Until his death in 1970 he continued to act as Cukor's colour consultant. Their images were inspired by certain panoramic paintings where a single detail becomes a focal point. Thus Cukor exploited wide screen and colour to achieve various striking effects: the smoky colours of the band framing Garland during 'The Man That Got Away'; the mirrors,

A Star is Born

magnifying glasses and implements that fill the frame to turn a make-up department into a virtual Universal horror set; the morose clown figures glimpsed at the sides of the screen in the backstage sequences.

Cukor's conception of the musical, however, was always 'naturalistic', in the sense that numbers should ideally be a part of the plot, springing from it as opposed to interrupting it. (Thus his few musicals are mainly about show-people). The producers saw fit to insert the long, more fantastical number, 'Born in a Trunk', in an effort to counteract Cukor's conception and to give the public what it thought they wanted from a musical. This resulted, however, in a loss of 27 minutes of Cukor's material, including the number 'Lose That Long Face'.

Despite the obvious commerical success of the inserted sequence, Cukor's own use of the musical number works well in the film on a more intimate, level. 'Somewhere There's a Someone', for example, is a song Esther sings for Norman in their own living room, mocking the

big production number she has been rehearsing at the studio. It springs directly from the dynamics of the plot, working both as a critique of the genre itself and as an index of the state of the relationship between Esther and Norman. Norman is sitting at home, unemployed, when Esther returns from the studio, still wearing her rehearsal costume, and puts on the practice record. Using household props – chairs, lamps, trollies and

cushions – she unconsciously attempts to 'domesticate' the number in order to reduce the importance of her professional role. There is a clash between public and private worlds, as well as between assigned roles (Norman remains a passive spectator throughout the sequence). It is a stunning fusion of elements – domestic melodrama and musical – that is typical of the way the film works as a whole.

MARTIN SUTTON

Directed by George Cukor, 1954
Prod co: Transcona Enterprises. **prod:** Sidney Luft. **assoc prod:** Vern Alves. **sc:** Moss Hart, from the films *A Star Is Born* (1937) by Dorothy Parker, Alan Campbell, Robert Carson, William A. Wellman, and *What Price Hollywood?* (1932) by Adela Rogers St John. **photo** (Technicolor, CinemaScope): Sam Leavitt. **special colour consultant:** Hoyningen-Huene. **sp eff:** H.F. Koenekamp. **ed:** Folmar Blangsted. **art dir:** Malcolm Bert. **cost:** Jean Louis, Mary Ann Nyberg. **mus dir:** Ray Heindorf. **songs:** Harold Arlen, Ira Gershwin, Leonard Gershe. **chor:** Richard Barstow. **sd:** Charles B. Lang, David Forrest. **add sequence dir** ('Born in a Trunk'): Richard Barstow, Roger Edens. **r/t:** 182 minutes, then 154 minutes, finally 135 minutes.
Cast: Judy Garland (*Vicki Lester*), James Mason (*Norman Maine*), Jack Carson (*Matt Libby*), Charles Bickford (*Oliver Niles*), Tom Noonan (*Danny McGuire*), Lucy Marlow (*Lola Lavery*), Amanda Blake (*Susan*), Irving Bacon (*Graves*), Hazel Shermet (*Miss Wheeler*), James Brown (*Glenn Williams*).

Esther Blodgett, singer with the Glenn Williams band, first meets film star Norman Maine at a charity gala. He is drunk and interrupts her act while she is singing 'You Gotta Have Me Go With You' (1). Even his publicity manager Matt Libby has difficulty restraining him.

Norman is captivated and next tracks her down to a small club where she is rehearsing a number – 'That Man That Got Away' (2). He says she is a great artist and persuades her to take a screen test. This is a success (3), she is renamed Vicki Lester and makes a trial musical sequence, 'Born in a Trunk' (4).

As her career takes off, Esther and Norman marry secretly (5), but his career falters and his drinking increases. He becomes depressed, despite her attempts to cheer him up (such as belittling her own achievements in the musical parody 'Somewhere There's a Someone').

At an Oscar ceremony (6), he embarrasses everyone by interrupting the proceedings and asking for a job (7). After a visit to a sanitorium and an appearance in court (8), Norman finally drowns himself in the sea one morning (9-production shot) in front of their home. Esther goes into mourning, but returns to showbusiness, announcing herself proudly as 'Mrs Norman Maine' (10-production shot) at the start of the show.

1

4

JAMES DEAN NATALIE WOOD SAL MINEO

in Warner Bros.

"REBEL WITHOUT A CAUSE"

CINEMASCOPE
and WARNERCOLOR

...and they both come from 'good' families!

Directed by Nicholas Ray, 1955
Prod co: Warner Bros. **prod:** David Weisbart. **sc:** Stewart Stern, Irving Shulman, from a story by Nicholas Ray. **photo:** Ernest Haller. **ed:** William Zeigler. **art dir:** Malcolm Bart. **mus dir:** Leonard Rosenman. **r/t:** 111 minutes.
Cast: James Dean (*Jim*), Natalie Wood (*Judy*), Jim Backus (*Jim's father*), Ann Doran (*Jim's mother*), Rochelle Hudson (*Judy's mother*), William Hopper (*Judy's father*), Sal Mineo (*Plato*), Corey Allen (*Buzz*), Dennis Hopper (*Goon*), Edward Platt (*Ray*), Steffi Sidney (*Mil*), Marietta Canty (*maid*), Ian Wolfe (*lecturer*), Frank Mazzola (*Crunch*).

When *Rebel Without a Cause* was premiered in Britain, in January 1956, the British critics considered it well-made, but some reviewers sustained severe moral outrage. *The Spectator* said:

'Its solemnity is rather irritating, seeing that a few good spanks would settle a lot of its problems.'
The *Daily Sketch* critic praised Nicholas Ray's direction but warned: 'That kind of brilliance in this kind of picture can be dangerous.'

Rebel Without a Cause is, of course, a 'problem picture' in the honourable Warner's tradition and can trace its ancestry back through the Dead End Kids' movies and *Angels With Dirty Faces* (1938) to the founding principles of 'social conscience' drama. In the wake of location-shot thrillers like *Gun Crazy* (1949) and alongside con-

temporary 'teenpix' – B movies like *Five Against the House* (1955) – *Rebel Without a Cause* looks even more like the 'realist' romance it is. But Nicholas Ray and screenwriter Stewart Stern made determined efforts to accommodate a documentary feel within the parameters of the high-gloss, A-feature production values required at Warners.

Ray and Stern spent weeks interviewing youth leaders and juvenile officers. They sat in on juvenile court sessions and spoke with criminologists including one who had been the chief psychiatrist at the Nuremberg trials. They did their homework.

The scenario, as Eric Rohmer observed in the French magazine of film theory *Cahiers du Cinéma* in 1955, falls neatly into the five acts of classical tragedy: exposition, with the conflict between the parents

and the children clearly stated; act two, in which Jim befriends Plato and is taunted by Buzz; act three, which includes the 'chicken run' with its fatal climax; act four, where Jim and Judy enjoy a transitory peace and share their love with Plato; and the final tragic act whose full impact is engraved on Jim's anguished face. As befits Aristotle's rules, the action is all but contained within 24 hours.

With that kind of narrative compression, the film could have emerged as hysterical melodrama, but even in the emotionally climactic scene of the domestic quarrel, the audience is never allowed to assume a dispassionate, 'objective' perspective. 'We are all involved!' as Jim exclaims. Ray's direction is in control: his camera spins upright out of a brilliant inverted shot from Jim's viewpoint. He then forces the action of the argument across the room and back against the stairs for greater dramatic effect and intercuts low-angle, high-angle and obliquely distorted shots to disrupt the perspective that the viewer normally considers his or her privilege. It is a bravura piece of direction in a film whose *mise-en-scène* is elsewhere distinguished by set-pieces, like the 'chicken run' and the final planetarium scenes – both of which are staged under the artificial, theatrical lighting of a circle of car headlamps.

The real director of *Rebel Without a Cause*, however, may be James Dean, in the sense that the film critic David Thomson describes him 'redirecting the picture by virtue of sheer presence'. If the complex experience of reading a film can be premised on the *look* constantly exchanged between the

viewer and the on-screen protagonists, then *direction* may be construed as the control and orientation of that look. The unique qualities of James Dean as an actor, especially in the intuitive relationship he shared with Nicholas Ray, permit the 'lingering' of the look (Dean's characteristic pauses) and provoke the disorientation of the look (his restlessness in the CinemaScope frame). In short, Dean tells us where to look and what to notice.

In the scene where Jim meets Judy outside her house at night, we anticipate the confirmation of the love between them and, therefore, might expect a progression from individual close-ups, to two-shot, to embrace. Instead, shooting in medium close-up, Ray shows Jim, agitated, lolling or rolling over, dominating the central and left areas of the vast CinemaScope image; while Judy remains almost motionless right of frame. The framing, like everything else in the film, privileges Dean, confirming his dominance and suggesting that Ray was taking advantage of this opportunity to play Dean as his *alter ego* and extend the art of directing through performance so that Dean can be seen as acting out Ray's romantic fantasy. To quote David Thomson again:

'Arguably only Nicholas Ray could have given Dean a part that guessed at the looming alienation in America.'

Dean and Ray were two loners from Middle America, down there in the comfortable (studio-set) suburban homes, who fled to the wide-open spaces of a mansion in the hills and an observatory that showed moving pictures of the heavens.
MARTYN AUTY

2

3

5

6

7

8

9

Jim, the adolescent son of middle-class parents recently moved to California, is run in for drunkeness by the police (1). He sobers up and has a sympathetic hearing from the juvenile-offenders officer (2).

The following day, Jim's first day at his new high school, he meets Judy and her gang of rowdy friends. In the course of a school visit to the local planetarium, Jim becomes friendly with Plato, an unbalanced, orphaned kid seeking affection. Outside the planetarium Jim is taunted into a fight with Buzz (3), the leader of the pack and Judy's boyfriend. They agree to meet later that evening for a 'chicken run' – an endurance test in which each will drive an old car to the cliff edge and leap clear at the last possible moment.

Seeking, but failing to get, advice from his father, Jim joins Buzz at the rendezvous (4). They line up (5), Judy signals the start of the race and the cars head for the cliff-edge. Buzz's sleeve catches in the doorhandle causing him to go over the edge with the car. Jim consoles Judy and drives her home.

Jim feels he must go to the police but his parents object: a violent quarrel ensues (6). However, Jim goes to the police station and is seen by Buzz's gang-mates (7). They swear to get even with him.

Picking up Judy on the way, Jim drives to a large deserted house in the hills where they are joined by Plato (8). Jim and Judy declare their love (9). Buzz's gang follow them there and beat up Plato who nevertheless manages to shoot one of them. The police arrive and chase Plato to the planetarium.

Jim finally persuades the frightened Plato to give himself up but, at the crucial moment, shots are fired from the police cordon and Plato falls down. An anguished Jim zips up the jacket on his friend's body and escorts Judy from the scene.

Right: setting up the final scene in which Plato is lured from the planetarium to his death

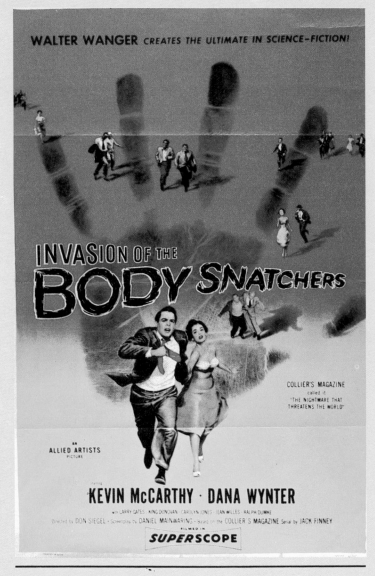

Directed by Don Siegel, 1956
Prod co: Allied Artists. **prod:** Walter Wanger. **sc:** Daniel Mainwaring, from a story by Jack Finney. **photo** (Superscope): Ellsworth Fredericks. **ed:** Robert S. Eisen. **art dir:** Ted Haworth. **mus:** Carmen Dragon. **r/t:** 80 minutes.
Cast: Kevin McCarthy (*Dr Miles Bennell*), Dana Wynter (*Becky Driscoll*), Larry Gates (*Dr Danny Kauffman*), King Donovan (*Jack*), Carolyn Jones (*Theodora*), Jean Willes (*Sally*), Ralph Dumke (*Nick*), Virginia Christine (*Wilma*), Tom Fadden (*Uncle Ira*), Kenneth Patterson (*Mr Driscoll*), Whit Bissell (*psychiatrist*), Richard Deacon (*doctor at hospital*), Guy Way (*policeman*), Sam Peckinpah (*man*).

The year 1956 saw the release of *The Ten Commandments*, *Around the World in 80 Days* and *War and Peace* – star-studded block-busters with massive budgets splashed over gigantic screens. Television and cinema battled for audiences for their money, and maybe also for their minds. . . .

Only two years previously the McCarthy witch-hunts had come to an end, and though the humiliation and degradation which had ruined many lives and careers was over, the distasteful memory lingered on. Nowhere is this better reflected than in Don Siegel's *Invasion of the Body Snatchers* – an 80-minute, black-and-white, low budget production, with no stars, that remains one of the most intelligent science-fiction movies of all time.

In outline the film is classic sci-fi,

with alien powers taking over the human form and mind, and replacing them with blank, emotionless subservience. Its hero is, of course, the exception: the individual who refuses to submit, only to discover that his friends, neighbours and the authorities have all been taken over. His gradual realization of what is happening and his attempts to escape from a seemingly inevitable fate set *Body Snatchers* in the pattern of the classic thriller and of such later Don Siegel films as *Coogan's Bluff* (1968), *Dirty Harry* (1971), *Charley Varrick* (1973) and, most recently, *Escape from Alcatraz* (1979). Although *Body Snatchers* is his only sci-fi piece, it is certainly not his only movie whose central character is a rebel, an outsider who runs against society's grain. Indeed, in the 1954 prison

drama *Riot in Cell Block 11*, he had already begun to develop the theme.

His producer on both occasions was Walter Wanger – undoubtedly one of Hollywood's better independent producers. For *Foreign Correspondent* (1940) Wanger employed Hitchcock; for *The Long Voyage Home* (1940) and *Stagecoach* (1939) he used the talents of John Ford; and between 1937 and 1948 Fritz Lang made three films for him. However, in the case of *Invasion of the Body Snatchers* Wanger was cast as the villain of the piece, or more precisely the pieces at the beginning and end of the movie. Neither the prologue, in which Miles tries to persuade the cops that the aliens are taking over, nor the epilogue, in which he is proved right, were approved by Siegel. They add nothing to the movie, and since they mean that the story is told in flashback, much of the final tension is destroyed by the knowledge that Miles has in fact reached the outside world.

That they do not destroy the film entirely is not only a tribute to Siegel's direction, but also to a masterly piece of screenwriting by Daniel Mainwaring, who also wrote *The Hitchhiker* (1953) and *The Phenix City Story* (1955).

Mainwaring transformed the original story, by veteran science-fiction writer Jack Finney, into part of his own continuing vision of America as a society riddled with urban paranoia and ever-growing political hysteria. Despite a brush with Hollywood's witch hunters, and being fired by RKO studio-boss Howard Hughes as politically suspect, Mainwaring continued to write. His later work included two more screenplays for Don Siegel, *Baby Face Nelson* (1957) and *The Gun Runners* (1958), but it was in *Body Snatchers* that he perfectly captured the feel of small-town America, isolated and menacing to

any outsider who is not part of its threatening landscape.

In this he was supported by uniformly excellent ensemble acting: neither Kevin McCarthy nor Dana Wynter were ever big stars but their solid professionalism is convincing enough. One treat is King Donovan as Miles' friend Jack, but the real curiosity is the name Sam Peckinpah at the bottom of the supporting-cast credits. In an interview Don Siegel revealed that it was out of personal friendship that Peckinpah, then down on his luck, was put on the payroll, but yes he actually does appear, albeit indistinctly.

In 1978 it was Siegel's turn to make a guest appearance, as a taxi driver, in Philip Kaufman's remake of Siegel's own film. The new version had stars (Donald Sutherland, Leonard Nimoy), colour, a much larger budget, more locations and more explicitly horrific special effects than were permissible in 1956. Yet its highlight is Kevin McCarthy charging into Sutherland's car and screaming the same message that he had delivered over twenty years earlier.

In complete contrast to the remake, the power of Siegel's movie lies in its simplicity – one of the most powerfully disturbing and chilling moments in all cinema is when Miles wakes Becky, and a kiss reveals the cold reality that she has finally been taken over by the aliens. In a 1968 interview with Peter Bogdanovich, Don Siegel described *Invasion of the Body Snatchers* as 'probably my finest film. I think that the world is populated by pods and I wanted to show them.' A quarter of a century later the dramatic realization of that statement remains undiminished.

PETER HOWDEN

Below: acting their way out of a tight corner – Kevin McCarthy and Dana Wynter receive final instructions from Don Siegel

1

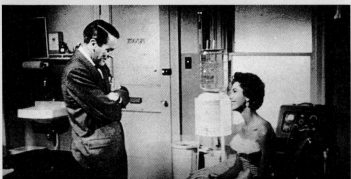

2

Los Angeles. A young man is frantically trying to convince the authorities (1) that an invasion is taking place in the small community of Santa Mira – an invasion by an alien force of 'pods' which have the power to completely take over the minds and bodies of local inhabitants.

In flashback the man – a young doctor named Miles Bennell – tells of a curious outbreak of cases in which people are reported to have changed and no longer seem 'real'. Miles strikes up a relationship with a young divorcee, Becky (2), and their fears prove justified when a friend, Jack, shows them a half-formed 'blank' of himself that he has discovered (3). Later that evening Jack's pod comes alive; Jack and his wife Teddy run over to tell Miles; he, suddenly fearing for Becky's life, rushes to her home and discovers a Becky pod in the basement (4). He finds the real Becky in a coma-like sleep and carries her away to safety.

The next evening, while at a barbecue party at Teddy and Jack's, Miles walks into the greenhouse and discovers four exploding pods containing blanks of Miles, Becky, Jack and Teddy (5). Miles and Becky drive off into the night – only to discover that a gas-station attendant has put two pods in the boot of their car. It becomes apparent that the people of Santa Mira (6) are being taken over by the pods while they sleep. Soon Miles and Becky are the only real people left. Tired, but not daring to sleep, they escape to the countryside (7).

Succumbing to sleep, Becky's mind is taken over. Miles, pursued by the aliens, carries on running until he reaches the highway (8).

The story switches to the present. Miles' story is disbelieved until someone comes in to report an accident involving a lorry filled with large pods . . .

3

4

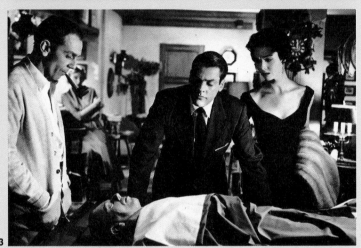

5

6

7

8

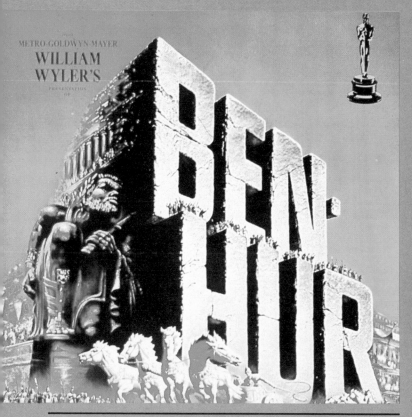

METRO-GOLDWYN-MAYER
WILLIAM WYLER'S
PRESENTATION OF

BEN-HUR

Directed by William Wyler, 1959

Prod co: MGM. **prod:** Sam Zimbalist. **sc:** Karl Tunberg from *A Tale of Christ* by General Lew Wallace. **photo:** (Technicolor, Camera 65): Robert L. Surtees. **sp photo eff:** A. Arnold Gillespie, Lee LeBlanc, Rober R. Hoag. **ed:** Ralph E. Winters, John D. Dunning. **art dir:** William A. Horning, Edward Carfagno. **set dir:** Hugh Hunt. **mus:** Miklós Rózsa. **cost:** Elizabeth Haffenden. **sd:** Franklin Milton. **2nd unit dir:** Andrew Marton, Yakima Canutt, Mario Soldati. **2nd unit photo:** Piero Portulupi. **3rd unit dir:** Richard Thorpe. **3rd unit photo:** Harold E. Wellman. **r/t:** 217 mins. World premiere, State Theatre New York, 18 November 1959.
Cast: Charlton Heston (*Judah Ben-Hur*), Stephen Boyd (*Messala*), Haya Harareet (*Esther*), Jack Hawkins (*Quintus Arrius*), Hugh Griffith (*Sheikh Ilderim*), Martha Scott (*Miriam*), Cathy O'Donnell (*Tirzah*), Frank Thring (*Pontius Pilate*). Sam Jaffe (*Simonides*), Finlay Currie (*Balthazar*), Terence Longdon (*Drusus*), George Relph (*Tiberius*), Adi Berber (*Malluch*), Laurence Payne (*Joseph*), André Morell (*Sextus*), Marina Berti (*Flavia*), Claude Heater (*Christ*), John Le Mesurier (*doctor*), Stella Vitelleschi (*Amrah*), Jose Greci (*Mary*), John Horsley (*Spintho*), Richard Coleman (*Metallus*), Duncan Lamont (*Marius*), Ralph Truman (*aide to Tiberius*), Robert Brown (*chief-of-rowers*).

With its current worldwide gross exceeding $80 million and its still unbeaten 11 Academy Awards, *Ben-Hur* is one of the most successful films of all time. It is the Hollywood epic *par excellence*.

Made at Cinecittà Studios in Rome for $15 million, *Ben-Hur* was then the most expensive film ever made. MGM had previously filmed the story in 1925. It was a production beset by difficulties that, owing to its massive cost, failed to show a profit but which was a milestone in cinema history. The 1959 film was a make-or-break venture for MGM and they entrusted it to the fastidious William Wyler, who had worked briefly on the silent version.

If some of the film's spectacle is betrayed by unconvincing model and matte shots, the chariot race (co-directed by Andrew Marton and the ace stuntman Yakima Canutt) is deservedly celebrated as the most thrilling action sequence ever filmed. Early in the film, Ben Hur gives Messala a white horse as a token of their friendship, but from that moment Messala becomes the film's electrifying villain, casting a dark shadow over the whole story. The race is the great symbolic ritual of the narrative as Judah Ben-Hur's white horses run neck-and-neck with Messala's blacks.

It is a tribute to Wyler's narrative skill and to the intense performances by Charlton Heston, as Judah Ben-Hur, and Stephen Boyd, as Messala, that the race does not render the final hour an anti-climax. Despite the towering sets and thronging extras we never lose sight of the human drama. Judah might win the race but, as the dying Messala says, 'the race goes on'. At this point, Judah's victory seems as elusive as ever.

The novel, by General Lew Wallace and first published in 1880, exists within the branch of Victorian fiction which presents the reader with a daunting fresco of characters and sub-plots resolved only by dramatic coincidences. The film's literate and often poetic screenplay – credited to Karl Tunberg, but co-written with the playwright Christopher Fry and the novelist Gore Vidal – eliminates Wallace's padding but retains the Victorian elements of melodrama and divine intervention.

'There are many paths of God, my son', says Balthazar to Judah, 'I hope yours will not be too difficult.' In fact, Judah's path is extremely difficult, involving the moral and physical challenges all classical heroes must endure. Judah's destiny is to become a believer at the Crucifixion and the cross itself becomes a compelling structural motif. Most obviously there is the cross-beam into which Judah and Messala throw their javelins – less obviously there are the three nails in the wall at which Judah prays before the race – and the paths of the characters within each stage of the story repeat the pattern.

After the race Esther snaps to Judah, 'It's as though you have become Messala!' and to underline the point Judah is subsequently seen resisting his destiny by ignoring the Sermon on the Mount, claiming he has 'business with Rome'. The imagery here, with Judah and Jesus occupying the same frame but with an immense distance between them, is epical in the purest sense.

At another point Balthazar mistakes Judah for Jesus and indeed, one can interpret Judah, Messala and Jesus as facets of a single character: Judah's life is saved by Messala, then by Jesus; Judah takes Messala's life and Jesus dies to 'save us all'. In another way the Roman Quintus Arrius and the Wise Man Balthazar are basically the same character, both searching – from pagan and Christian perspectives – for divine guidance and both adopting Judah as their son.

All the characters and episodes are linked in this way and by Wyler's extensive use of water to signify purification. This culminates in the moment when the blood from the cross is gradually dispersed by the rain, heralding a new beginning.

The subtleties of such details are unusual for a film on this scale, as are the varieties of mood and emotion. On the one hand there are sweeping dramatic moments – the race, the prolonged argument between Judah and Messala, the uplifting sequence when Judah is given water by Jesus and later when the scene is reversed on the road to Calvary. On the other hand there are moments of extraordinary warmth and intimacy – the tentative love scene between Esther and Judah, and Balthazar gazing into the night sky ablaze with stars, wondering what became of the child he saw born in Bethlehem. Therefore, even though the spectacular chariot race made *Ben-Hur* famous, it is nonetheless highly valued for a multitude of other reasons.

ADRIAN TURNER

2

3

5

6

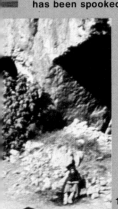

8

9

In Jerusalem the newly appointed Roman Tribune Messala meets his childhood friend Judah Ben-Hur, a Jewish aristocrat, and asks his help in eliminating rebellion (1). Judah refuses and his friendship with Messala suddenly ends. When the Roman Governor is injured in a fall after his horse has been spooked by a tile which falls from Judah's roof, Messala declaims Judah as a rebel and imprisons his mother and sister. In chains and dying of thirst, Judah is given water by a carpenter's son (2). Condemned to the galleys (3). Judah saves the life of the Roman Consul Quintus Arrius during a sea battle (4–5). The grateful Quintus Arrius takes Judah to Rome and adopts him as his son (6).

Returning to Jerusalem after seven years, Judah arrives at his old home, now neglected and overgrown, and is reunited with Esther, whom he loves, and her father, steward to the House of Hur. In a chariot race (7) Judah takes revenge on Messala (8) who, on his death-bed (9), tells Judah to look for his mother and sister in the Valley of the Lepers (10). Esther persuades Judah to take them to Jesus of Nazareth. They arrive at his trial. Recognising the Nazarene (11), Judah attends the Crucifixion and returning home he finds his mother and sister cured (12).

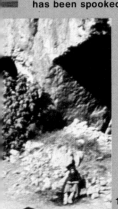

11

12

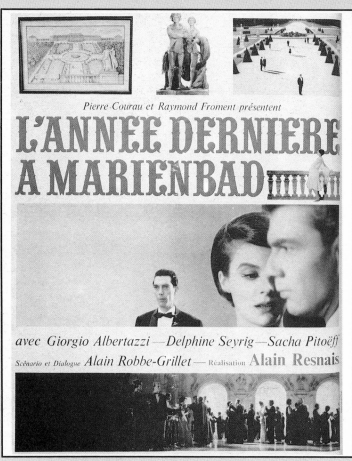

Pierre Courau et Raymond Froment présentent

L'ANNÉE DERNIÈRE A MARIENBAD

1

avec Giorgio Albertazzi — Delphine Seyrig — Sacha Pitoëff

Scénario et Dialogue Alain Robbe-Grillet — *Réalisation* **Alain Resnais**

LAST YEAR IN MARIENBAD

4

What really happened 'last year in Marienbad'? Rarely has critical speculation over a film's content been so active. It was reported that not even the director, Alain Resnais, and the writer, Alain Robbe-Grillet, were in complete agreement. Resnais claimed that an encounter had occurred the previous year while Robbe-Grillet declared that one sometimes had the impression that the whole episode was a figment of the narrator's imagination. But perhaps this much-publicized divergence of views was a calculated ploy, a hint to the spectator as to how the film should be approached – that is, with no preconceived idea. One eminent French critic, Jacques Brunius, declared unequivocally after several viewings that it was the greatest film ever made; others dismissed it as a pretentious art-movie spoof. One thing is certain: a true appreciation of the film calls for the audience's complete surrender to its unique form and mood.

The first voice to be heard is that of the narrator, faintly and then more clearly, as the camera examines the furnishings of a vast, baroque hotel with its endless, empty corridors, numbered rooms, ornate ceilings and glittering mirrors. The voice intones: 'Once again I walk, once again, along these corridors, across these salons, these galleries, in this edifice from another century . . .' In one of the great salons an audience sits motionless, watching a play. 'And now,' says the on-stage actress, 'I am yours'. The curtain falls. The play's conclusion prefigures the final surrender of the film's heroine.

Gradually, through snatches of overheard conversations, shots of curiously posed single figures or static groups, the film establishes its disturbing world, which might be dream or stylized reality. The three central characters start to reveal their identities: the melancholy woman who is staying in the hotel with a gaunt-faced man who may, or may not, be her husband and an insinuating stranger, the narrator, who claims that the woman agreed a year ago to meet him again now.

She denies all knowledge of him or previous acquaintanceship but the stranger relentlessly pursues his detailed tactic of persuasion. Does she not recall the time when, while walking through the garden, she slipped and broke off the heel of her shoe? Later on, when they are walking together, she stumbles and grabs his arm for support. This is seen in long-shot and it is uncertain whether she actually breaks the heel. Is this the scene that, according to his claim, happened in the past, or a re-enactment, or history repeating itself? In this delicate fusion between past and present

nothing can ever be quite certain.

Several questions suggest themselves. Is this strange château, set in its formal gardens, an exclusive nursing home and is the stranger perhaps the woman's psychoanalyst, striving to make her recall a past emotional experience which she has unconsciously blocked from her memory? And her clothes, quintessential expression of outré Parisian chic by Chanel . . . do they provide a clue? It seems that in general a white dress is worn for scenes in the past and black for the present – but not quite consistently. What about the

7

3

2

5

6

shadowy figure of the man who 'may be her husband' . . . husband? lover? brother? He is frequently seen playing a pre-ordained match-stick game which he invariably wins. Usually it is the stranger whom he defeats.

At one point, when the stranger seems almost on the verge of forcing the woman to admit the reality of the past events he describes and has left the couple alone, she turns to her 'husband' and begs him, with a hint of desperation, not to leave her. His reply is reasoned and cool: 'But it is you who are leaving me – you know that!' When his prediction proves true, she departs with no sense of joy or fulfilment; she seems rather to have left her haven for an unknown destination. In this contest of wills and persuasion she appears to be the victim of an inexorable fate, possibly leading to her death or some kind of oblivion.

The eternal fascination of Last Year in Marienbad is that each time the spectator feels sure of having grasped the key to its sphinx-like riddle, it presents another aspect to disprove his theory. Though not completely convincing, the theory of the recurrent dream is worth considering. The obsessive nature of such dreams still allows for some

measure of improvisation of the events to suit the dreamer's fancy; they can incorporate acceptance and rejection of particular elements – even adjusted replays.

When, for example, the woman asks the stranger to leave her alone, he leans against a balustrade which crumbles under the pressure. There is a quick cutaway. This must surely be a moment of fantasy and when the balustrade is next seen it ought to be intact. But it is still broken! Does this reflect the dreamer's unshakeable conviction that the event actually occurred? Is it not more likely to be the woman's wish-fulfilment, a persistent longing to rid herself of the importunate stranger. On reflection, the second explanation is more plausible. But with everything in this enigmatic film it is a matter of 'I think so'; never 'I know for sure'.

On further inspection, Last Year in Marienbad, with its subtle clues, its intricate juggling with past and present, its depiction of a reality that might be dream or of a dream with a hallucinatory hint of reality, takes on the aspect of a masterly detective story. The figures – for they are figures rather than personages – are moved through their

exquisitely controlled paces by a director who demonstrates the precision of a master chess player. Its enclosed world has the mesmeric

quality of a superior fairy-tale with, like many of the most haunting fairy-tales, a touch of veiled menace.   DEREK PROUSE

Directed by Alain Resnais, 1961
Prod co: Terra-Film/Société Nouvelle des Films Cormoran/Précitel/Como-Films/Les Films Tamara/Cinetel/Silver Films (Paris)/Cineriz (Rome). **prod:** Pierre Courau (Précitel), Raymond Froment (Terra-Film). **sc:** Alain Robbe-Grillet. **photo:** Sacha Vierny (Dyaliscope). **ed:** Henri Colpi, Jasmine Chasney. **art dir:** Jacques Saulnier. **mus:** Francis Seyrig. **cost:** Chanel, Bernard Evein. **sd:** Guy Villette. **r/t:** 94 minutes. World premiere: Venice Film Festival, 29 August 1961. Released in the USA and GB as *Last Year in Marienbad*.
Cast: Delphine Seyrig (*A*), Giorgio Albertazzi (*X*), Sacha Pitoëff (*M*), Françoise Bertin, Luce Garcia-Ville, Héléna Kornel, Françoise Spira, Karin Toeche-Mittler, Pierre Barbaud, Wilhelm Von Deek, Jean Lanier, Gérard Lorin, Davide Montemuri, Gilles Quéant, Gabriel Werner.

A vast, grandiose hotel, set in formal grounds, is sparsely peopled with guests standing around in statuesque poses (1) or static conversation groups, watching an obscure drama (2) or playing an apparently simple game (3). The hotel provides the setting for a strange encounter: a beautiful woman, A, staying there with M, who is possibly her husband (4), is approached by a man, X (5). He claims that they had had a close relationship here the previous year, when they had

arranged to meet again a year thence with the intention of going away together (6). She denies all knowledge of this (7). But he assails her with such persuasive detail (8) of their shared experience that her resistance crumbles and he prevails upon her to leave with him. She sits rigidly in her bedroom awaiting the stroke of midnight before joining him at the appointed rendezvous outside, from which she can see the hotel she is leaving forever (9).

8

9

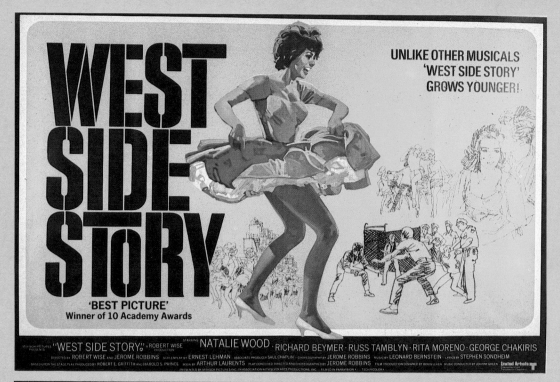

WEST SIDE STORY

'BEST PICTURE'
Winner of 10 Academy Awards

UNLIKE OTHER MUSICALS
'WEST SIDE STORY'
GROWS YOUNGER!

MIRISCH PICTURES PRESENTS "WEST SIDE STORY" A ROBERT WISE PRODUCTION STARRING NATALIE WOOD RICHARD BEYMER · RUSS TAMBLYN · RITA MORENO · GEORGE CHAKIRIS DIRECTED BY ROBERT WISE AND JEROME ROBBINS SCREENPLAY BY ERNEST LEHMAN ASSOCIATE PRODUCER SAUL CHAPLIN CHOREOGRAPHY BY JEROME ROBBINS MUSIC BY LEONARD BERNSTEIN LYRICS BY STEPHEN SONDHEIM BOOK BY ARTHUR LAURENTS PLAY CONCEIVED DIRECTED AND CHOREOGRAPHED BY JEROME ROBBINS FILM PRODUCTION DESIGNED BY BORIS LEVEN MUSIC CONDUCTED BY JOHNNY GREEN United Artists BASED UPON THE STAGE PLAY PRODUCED BY ROBERT E. GRIFFITH AND HAROLD S. PRINCE PRESENTED BY MIRISCH PICTURES, INC. IN ASSOCIATION WITH SEVEN ARTS PRODUCTIONS, INC. FILMED IN PANAVISION 70° • TECHNICOLOR

Directed by Robert Wise, Jerome Robbins, 1961
Prod co: Mirisch/Seven Arts. **prod:** Robert Wise. **assoc prod:** Saul Chaplin. **sc:** Ernest Lehman, based on the stage production by Robert E. Griffith, Harold S. Prince, from the book by Arthur Laurents. **photo** (Technicolor, Panavision 70): Daniel L. Fapp. **sp eff:** Linwood Dunn. **ed:** Thomas Stanford, Marshall M. Borden. **art dir:** Boris Leven, M. Zuberano. **titles:** Saul Bass. **cost:** Irene Sharaff. **mus:** Leonard Bernstein. **mus dir:** Johnny Green. **mus arr:** Sid Ramin. **mus ed:** Richard Carruth. **lyr:** Stephen Sondheim. **chor:** Jerome Robbins. **sd:** Gilbert D. Marchant. **sd rec:** Murray Spivack, Fred Lau, Vinton Vernon. **prod man:** Allen K. Wood. **ass dir:** Robert E. Relyea. **r/t:** 152 minutes.
Cast: Natalie Wood (*Maria*), Richard Beymer (*Tony*), George Chakiris (*Bernardo*), Russ Tamblyn (*Riff*), Rita Moreno (*Anita*), Tony Mordente (*Action*), Tucker Smith (*Ice*), Simon Oakland (*Lieutenant Schrank*), William Bramley (*Officer Krupke*), Ned Glass (*Doc*), José De Vega (*Chino*), Sue Oakes (*Anybody's*), John Astin (*Glad Hand*), Penny Santon (*Madam Lucia*), Jay Norman (*Pepe*), Gus Trikonis (*Indio*), Robert Thompson (*Luis*), Eliot Field (*Baby John*), Larry Roquemore (*Rocco*), David Winters (*A-Rab*).

West Side Story begins even before the house-lights go down in the cinema. A long, low whistle fills the auditorium; the whistle is repeated; the lights go down and the film starts with a breathtaking aerial shot of Manhattan – a geometric display of crossing lines. Then the camera plunges to the streets below: a gang of youths walking along the road, clicking their fingers, keeping 'cool'; suddenly they freeze and move into a dance sequence. It is a daring and visually exciting opening to a film.

But more than that, these first few minutes establish a number of key elements: its location – the tenements and streets of Manhattan; its content – the rivalry between two gangs (one of white youths, one of Puerto Rican immigrants); and its form – a highly stylized musical. The opening prepares the audience for what is to follow.

West Side Story was conceived and developed for the stage by Jerome Robbins, who also choreographed and directed several of the dance routines. One of his early stage ballet hits was the choreography for Leonard

Bernstein's *Fancy Free* which later became the Broadway success *On the Town*. The film of *On the Town* (1949) had broken with tradition by attempting to integrate fully song, dance and dialogue into one continuous narrative, rejecting the often contrived excuses for breaking into song that had been a feature of previous musicals. However, it is relatively easy to do this when the plot of the film is nothing more than three sailors going ashore for 24 hours' leave, meeting three girls and returning to their ship.

West Side Story is a more difficult proposition. Loosely based on Shakespeare's *Romeo and Juliet*, it transposes the rivalry between the Capulet and Montague families to the tensions between racial groupings in New York, thus becoming one of the first musicals to deal with serious, contemporary issues – racialism and juvenile delinquency. The vigour and vitality of *West Side Story* owe a lot to its departure from the facile plots of *On the Town* or *Pal Joey* (1957) or the fantasy lives of *Seven Brides for Seven Brothers* (1954).

It presented Robbins and Robert Wise with the difficulty of how to carve out a modern style of presentation suitable for important problems. *West Side Story* found its style both by not trying to carry the plot forward in song and dance sequences – as *On the Town* did – and also by abandoning the hoedown set pieces of *Oklahoma!* (1955). Instead, the songs, at their best, add something more to the narrative, informing the audience about the atmosphere and details of the lives. The opening shots do this by economically establishing the territorial basis of the gangs' control. Later in the film, the aggressive and lively roof-top sequence 'America' is a hard-hitting proclamation of the disillusionment of immigrants with American society. On the other hand, the love song 'Maria' and the dance-hall routine, where the gangs challenge each other, are firmly part of the old tradition. **4**

Of the criticisms ranged against the film, one concerns its combination of naturalism through location shooting and the obvious stylization of studio work. Whereas the beginning was actually danced on the streets of New York, the 'rumble' takes place in a studio-constructed set. And the choice of Natalie Wood as Maria – she had to have her singing voice dubbed and had difficulty looking Puerto Rican – has also been questioned as giving the film an unreal texture. But *West Side Story* does not aim to be realistic: it is a modern parable of what *could* happen in a racially divided society.

With its combination of innovatory and traditional elements, this was very much a transitional musical. Bob Fosse took the techniques of *West Side Story* further when he brought serious issues to *Sweet Charity* (1969), and combined them with biting satire in *Cabaret* (1972). Robert Wise went on to **8**

direct his biggest success, another big-budget musical – *The Sound of Music* (1965). It needed other directors to see that there was a valuable exuberance and youthfulness that could be exploited to provide the material for even more exuberant and youth-orientated rock musicals of the next decade.

SALLY HIBBIN

On New York's West Side two gangs control the streets – the Jets (white teenagers) (1) and the

Sharks (Puerto Rican immigrants) (2). Riff, the leader of the Jets, tries to persuade Tony, who founded the gang but has since drifted away, to go to the local dance.

Maria, the sister of Bernardo who leads the Sharks, is excited about her first dance. She goes with Chino, Bernardo and his girlfriend Anita. When they arrive, the two gangs display their rivalry through the dances they perform (3). Tony enters and sees Maria:

they are both entranced (4). When he asks her to dance, Bernardo warns her that Tony is a member of the rival gang. Riff uses the incident as an excuse to propose a 'rumble'.

Tony visits Maria on the fire-escape outside her room (5) and they realize that, despite the difficulties, they love each other. Returning to Doc's shop (where he works) Tony finds a war council in session. He persuades them to have a fair fist fight

between representatives from each side.

Telling Bernardo that she will be working late (6), Maria stays at the dress-shop until Tony arrives. She persuades him to try and stop the fight, but when he gets to the 'rumble' his offer of friendship is misunderstood. Bernardo kills Riff (7), and Tony kills Bernardo. When the police turn up, the gangs scatter (8).

Learning of her brother's death, Maria decides to stand by Tony,

and begs Anita to take a message to him. Anita goes to Doc's but is insulted by the Jets; she then lies when she tells them that Chino has killed Maria in anger.

Desolate, Tony roams the streets calling for Chino to come and get him. He sees Maria too late: he has already been spotted by Chino who shoots him. Both gangs appear, and Maria, crying, accuses them all of Tony's death (9). They take Tony's body off, for once united in tragedy (10).

45

Directed by François Truffaut, 1962
Prod co: Les Films du Carrosse/SEDIF. **prod man:** Marcel Berbert. **sc:** François Truffaut, Jean Gruault, from the novel by Henri-Pierre Roché. **photo** (Franscope)**:** Raoul Coutard. **ed:** Claudine Bouché. **cost:** Fred Capel. **mus:** Georges Delerue. **song:** Boris Bassiak. **ass dir:** Georges Pellegrin, Robert Bober. **narr:** Michel Subor. **r/t:** 105 minutes. Paris premiere, 27 January 1962. Released in USA and GB as *Jules and Jim.*
Cast: Jeanne Moreau (*Catherine*), Oskar Werner (*Jules*), Henri Serre (*Jim*), Vanna Urbino (*Gilberte*), Boris Bassiak (*Albert*), Sabine Haudepin (*Sabine*), Marie Dubois (*Thérèse*), Jean-Louis Richard (*first customer in the café*), Michel Varesano (*second customer in the café*), Pierre Fabre (*drunkard in café*), Danielle Bassiak (*Albert's friend*), Bernard Largemains (*Merlin*), Elen Bober (*Mathilde*), Kate Noëlle (*Birgitta*), Anny Nielsen (*Lucy*), Christiane Wagner (*Helga*).

Based on a little-known autobiographical novel written by Henry-Pierre Roché when in his seventies, *Jules et Jim* was François Truffaut's third film and is still the one by which he is most affectionately known. Endlessly inventive and unquenchably high-spirited, it is one of those rare films which, after no more than a single viewing, inspire virtually total recall. Even its soundtrack continues to possess a naggingly memorable life of its own, thanks to Jeanne Moreau's breathy giggle, Oskar Werner's softly accented French and, not least, Georges Delerue's haunting theme music, which over the years has become almost the signature tune of the *nouvelle vague.*

Most astonishing of all, however, is the masterly ease with which, in this tale of an intermittently felicitous *ménage à trois,* Truffaut modulates between comedy (or rather, gaiety), drama and, ultimately, tragedy, while deploying a battery of perilously modish devices – jump cuts, freeze frames, nostalgic iris shots. His numerous imitators have managed only to hitch these techniques to the kind of broad comic romp of which Tony Richardson's *Tom Jones* (1963) might be the prototype. Though the triangle formed by Jules, Jim and the flighty, elusive Catherine is, in its restlessly shifting sympathies, anything but eternal and too often overcast to be considered unreservedly idyllic, none of the film's more sombre elements ever succeeds in snuffing out its youthful exuberance. For an example of how subtly it functions, one need look no further than Catherine herself, in Jeanne Moreau's enchanting and somehow 'definitive' performance. Rarely has the cinema invested one of its classic *femmes fatales* with such generous helpings of humour, charm and tenderness. Yet *fatale* she unquestionably is: figuratively, by the cavalier treatment which she metes out to her pair of suitors, capriciously switching her amorous attentions from one to the other and back again, even ditching both of them for the more immediately gratifying stimulation of an affair with a casual pick-up; and literally, at the end, when she nonchalantly drives Jim and herself headlong into the Seine. It is, above all, Catherine's mercurial femininity which has allowed the film to wear so much better than those sweatily explicit dramas of uncensored passion made during the same period (for instance, Jack Clayton's *Room at the Top,* 1959). Sex here is fun, at least on occasion. If the three protagonists fail to arrive at a workable 'design for living' no moral condemnation is implied by Truffaut: less unconventional relationships prove equally doomed.

Prior to their relationship with Catherine, the two Bohemian young men are so bewitched by the placidly mysterious features of a Greek goddess on a lantern slide that they promptly set off for the Adriatic to catch a glimpse of the original sculpture. Catherine, too, is an 'ideal' woman (the most perfectly realized, perhaps, in Truffaut's extensive gallery of portraits), all things to both men, separately or together – and the tragedy of the final suicide is not only her own and Jim's death, but the inconsolable solitude of Jules.

The balance between tragedy and comedy, so miraculously maintained throughout, derives also from the fact that, as the characters never physically age (though at the end Moreau sports granny glasses, the face behind them is just as radiantly, mischievously beautiful), it is from outside that the passage of time comes abruptly and cruelly to impinge on their intimate universe. World War I, evoked in newsreel footage that is startlingly stretched out to the full dimensions of the CinemaScope screen, causes the two friends to fear that one might kill the other (his name notwithstanding, Jules is German).

Then, suddenly, it is already 1933, as in a cinema the trio watch more newsreel footage of book-burning in Nazi Germany. And the advancing years are more benignly telegraphed by the ubiquitous Picasso paintings, passing through several stages of the artist's evolution. From the very beginning, however, the film has ominously hinted at the impermanence of their happiness: Catherine's first whimsical leap into the Seine; her ritualized burning of letters from past lovers ('old flames'), which almost results in her self-immolation; and the spectre of jealousy in a Rhineland chalet, a striking crane shot encapsulating both a nervously pacing Jim downstairs and Catherine and Jules romping ecstatically in the upstairs bedroom.

Of all the *nouvelle vague* directors, it is Truffaut alone who has carried on the tradition of French lyricism out of Vigo and Renoir despite once being its most vitriolic critic: in *Jules et Jim* his feeling for the countryside, sensuously captured by Raoul Coutard's ravishing black-and-white photography, is worthy – as is the whole film – of Renoir's *Une Partie de Campagne* (1936, A Day in the Country). And if Godard was without question the more revolutionary figure, it is surprisingly hard to imagine the course of contemporary cinema bereft of Truffaut's inimitable (though often imitated) delicacy and charm.   GILBERT ADAIR

Below: Truffaut discusses a point with Jeanne Moreau who gives a moving performance as the capricious Catherine

1

2

3

4

In pre-World War I Paris, two young men, the German Jules and Frenchman Jim, form an indestructible friendship (1). The situation changes however when Catherine, a beautiful but volatile young woman, enters their lives (2) and begins an affair with the diffident Jules (3).

They marry and, with their small daughter (4), settle in Germany; when war breaks out soon after, the once inseparable friends find themselves conscripted on opposite sides. After the war Jim, now a successful journalist in Paris, pays the couple a visit, during which he is deceived into believing that they are idyllically happy (5). But Jules sadly confesses in a letter that he is unable to hold on to Catherine and even encourages his friend, in a desperate attempt to keep his wife, to sleep with her (6).

Jim, no less defeated by her capricious moods and casual infidelity, soon returns to Paris and the passively loyal girlfriend, Gilberte, whom he had left behind. Several years pass. Jules and Catherine settle in Paris and the friends seem, on the surface, to have resumed their earlier relationship (7). But Jim, having recovered his independence, refuses to see it swallowed up once more in what he knows to be an unworkable situation. Whereupon the ever-inscrutable Catherine invites him into her car and drives them both into the Seine. Jules is left alone (8).

5

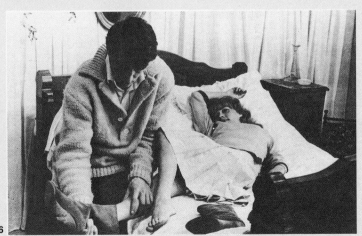

6

7

8

The whole world loves
Tom Jones!

X

ALBERT FINNEY SUSANNAH YORK
HUGH GRIFFITH EDITH EVANS
JOAN GREENWOOD *"Tom Jones"*
DIANE CILENTO

GEORGE DEVINE *and the guest appearance of* DAVID TOMLINSON JOHN OSBORNE TONY RICHARDSON EASTMAN COLOUR A WOODFALL PRODUCTION

Directed by Tony Richardson, 1963
Prod co: Woodfall (United Artists). **prod:** Tony Richardson. **exec prod:** Alan Kaplan. **sc:** John Osborne, based on the novel by Henry Fielding. **photo** (Eastman Colour): Walter Lassally. **2nd unit photo:** Manny Wynn. **ed:** Antony Gibbs. **art dir:** Ted Marshall, Ralph Brinton. **mus:** John Addison. **sd:** Don Challis. **prod sup:** Leigh Aman. **prod man:** Roy Millichip. **narr:** Micheál MacLiammóir. **r/t:** 128 minutes.
Cast: Albert Finney (*Tom Jones*), Susannah York (*Sophie Western*), Hugh Griffith (*Squire Western*), Edith Evans (*Miss Western*), Joan Greenwood (*Lady Bellaston*), Diane Cilento (*Molly Seagrim*), George Devine (*Squire Allworthy*), Joyce Redman (*Jenny Jones*), David Warner (*Blifil*), David Tomlinson (*Lord Fellamar*), Rosalind Knight (*Mrs Fitzpatrick*), Peter Bull (*Thwackum*), John Moffatt (*Square*), Patsy Rowlands (*Honour*), Wilfrid Lawson (*Black George*), Jack MacGowran (*Partridge*), Freda Jackson (*Mrs Seagrim*), Julian Glover (*Lt Northerton*), Rachel Kempson (*Bridget Allworthy*), George A. Cooper (*Fitzpatrick*), Angela Baddeley (*Mrs Wilkins*), Avis Bunnage (*landlady*), Rosalind Atkinson (*Mrs Miller*), James Cairncross (*Parson Supple*), Redmond Phillips (*Lawyer Dowling*), Mark Dignam (*lieutenant*), Lynn Redgrave (*Susan*), Jack Stewart (*MacLachlan*), Michael Brennan (*jailer*).

'The whole world loves Tom Jones!' proclaimed the posters hopefully, showing the title character with arms joyously outstretched as several scantily clad ladies worship at his feet. The slogan proved prophetic. Although it failed originally to obtain a circuit booking, *Tom Jones* broke box-office records when it opened at the London Pavilion – a success repeated when it was finally distributed across Britain and internationally. The film ultimately picked up four Oscars (for Best Film, Direction, Screenplay Adaptation and Music), as well as a host of festival and British Academy awards, and was universally received as one of the undisputed film delights of 1963.

Such commercial and critical acclaim might initially seem surprising. The film was based on one of those eighteenth-century literary classics more widely esteemed than read. Henry Fielding's comic novel contains much lively detail

and emphasizes the contrast between country and city – offering visual opportunities that the film wholeheartedly embraces. But both its episodic structure and digressive narrative style pose interpretative problems, and such unwieldy literary originals often spawn servile screen adaptations that sink under the weight of their own reverence.

Here, however, the treatment is at the hands of writer John Osborne and director Tony Richardson, and reverence is not a quality immediately associated with either of them. Osborne had rejuvenated the English stage in the late Fifties with plays such as *Look Back in Anger* and *Luther* – both celebrations of the rebel hero. Richardson had brought prestige to the British cinema with grim film versions of *A Taste of Honey* (1961) and *The Loneliness of the Long-Distance Runner* (1962). Whilst these truly abrasive personalities could not

be expected to match faithfully Fielding's urbane humour, it was fair to anticipate a sympathy with the unconventional hero and an identification with the novel's criticism of hypocrisy and humbug. Such expectations were amply fulfilled.

The film's success can be attributed to a combination of acting prowess, technical felicity and fortuitous timing. Certainly the film was fortunate in its cast, who all threw themselves into the period with energy and style. Also, if the distributors were dubious about the commercial potential of a period romp in a film era more noted for social realism, in retrospect it seems that it was precisely this novelty that attracted world audiences. *Tom Jones* brought colourful extravagance back into the British cinema – recalling the painterly style of Fielding's friend Hogarth – with its vigorous feeling for landscape and costume, while pointing out (in the celebrated stag-hunting scene) some of the century's lingering bestiality and barbarism.

This latter scene in particular reassured the critics. Even in period costume, Richardson and Osborne had not lost their cutting edge. Indeed, in some ways the film seemed to sharpen it, and Richardson found a perspective and wit sometimes absent from the dramas of British contemporary life made by him and other directors of the time. Tom Jones was Joe Lampton (ambitious working-class hero of *Room at the Top*, 1959) with a sense of humour: the underprivileged boy with sexual as well as social aspirations, shown in a way that reflected the increasingly liberated morality of the time – the England of 1745 and 1963 had suddenly come together. And in a strictly sexual

sense Tom Jones was a kind of rural James Bond. His appearance coincided with the emerging popularity of Bond, and the depiction of the hero's amorous appetites seemed to reflect a contemporary mood. The saucy sex comedy was hot property in 1963: if people could not get in to see *Tom Jones*, they went to see *Irma la Douce*.

The film was applauded for bringing a modern style – slapstick comedy, captions, narration, asides to the camera, speeded-up action – to a period classic: creating comedy out of the incongruity. Once the contemporary modishness had worn off, however, it became more common to claim that this style had little thematic justification. Also, as Tony Richardson's reputation subsequently declined, retrospective doubts were inevitably cast over his earlier achievements.

But if the whole world no longer loves *Tom Jones*, its impact at the time was enormous. It also blazed a trail of frankness and good cheer into the international market, epitomizing for many the sparkle and exuberance of swinging Britain in the Sixties. Its confidence and élan would be hard to reproduce today, and there is a whole world of difference between the jolly tread of Richardson's *Tom Jones* and the poisonous progress, a decade later, of Kubrick's *Barry Lyndon* (1975), also a dazzling re-creation of the eighteenth century, but which narrates the downfall of its eponymous social upstart with suave relish.

NEIL SINYARD

Tom Jones, abandoned as a baby in mysterious circumstances, is brought up by Squire Allworthy. Resented by Allworthy's legitimate heir Blifil, Tom grows into an amiable rascal, fond of poaching (1), hunting (2) and the fair sex. He loves Squire Western's daughter Sophie (3), but when discovered by his tutors with a local girl Molly, he gives them a thrashing and is banished by his benefactor. After numerous adventures he reaches London and embarks on an affair with the wealthy Lady Bellaston (5) whom he meets at a masque (6).

Meanwhile, Squire Western's sister has arranged a marriage between Sophie and Blifil (7). Horrified, Sophie escapes to London, meeting up with her cousin Mrs Fitzpatrick, who is also running away from her husband. Mr Fitzpatrick follows them and suspects Tom of having seduced his runaway wife.

Discovering Tom in London, Fitzpatrick involves him in a brawl (8). Tom wounds Fitzpatrick and is sentenced to be hanged (9) . . . largely on false evidence arranged by Blifil. However, Allworthy has discovered the truth about Tom's birth, concealed from him by Blifil – that Tom, though illegitimate, is the child not of a servant, but of Allworthy's sister Bridget. Tom is saved from the gallows and joyfully reunited with Sophie (10).

The director Joseph Losey first came across Robin Maugham's short novel *The Servant* in 1956 and immediately offered Dirk Bogarde the title role in the film version. The conniving manservant, so different from the parts that Bogarde had hitherto played, intrigued the actor but he and Losey finally decided that there was little chance of setting up the project in the censorious climate of the British cinema of that time. Six years later, the time was more propitious. (Bogarde, mainly a light comedy lead in the Fifties, had since shown considerable courage in changing his screen image by playing the homosexual laywer in *The Victim* 1961.)*The Servant*, already Pinteresque in its dark conflicts and veiled sexual overtones, was offered to Pinter who constructed his first screenplay from it.

But even with the combined names of Losey, Bogarde and Pinter, the project was not plain sailing. It was finally given the go-ahead on condition that it did not exceed a budget of £141,000. It didn't, and was in fact brought in slightly under budget – and became a big box-office success.

Ostensibly, the film depicts a reversal of power within a decaying class system: Tony is a relic of a monied, privileged class who has been brought up to assume that respect is unquestioningly due to him as a natural birthright; Barrett has trained himself in professional servitude – at the outset he is a kind of Admirable Crichton who can take smooth control of a situation which his betters have allowed to run to seed. But underneath his suave deference lurks a ruthless opportunism and he deploys his assets with infinite guile. When the decision has been taken to restore the house to its (presumably) former grandeur, it is he who suggests that mandarin and fuchsia are now considered to be a chic colour scheme, and subsequently takes over the whole redecoration. Swiftly and insidiously he has become the indispensable oracle of good taste.

Very soon, the house has become a candidate for a *House and Garden* illustration, but a house that is essentially sealed like a cocoon against the world outside. Douglas Slocombe's camera is there to record impeccably the activity and the detail within the transformed interior, acting almost as a *voyeur*: spying through bannisters at a revealing gesture or an unguarded expression; noting every rich gleam on polished wood or glittering mirrors, and every move in the game whereby the spineless owner is transformed into a fly enmeshed in a deceptively treacherous web.

From their first meeting when the servant discovers his employer sprawled in defenceless sleep in one of the drab rooms, it is clear that here is a proposition ripe for a take-over bid. Pinter's economic dialogue is capable of investing the most mundane reflection with a deadly undertone and, when the transition of power is finally, irrevocably made, a sado-masochistic

DIRK BOGARDE · SARAH MILES
WENDY CRAIG

THE SERVANT x

JAMES FOX

situation is exposed with shocking force. 'I couldn't get on without you', the erstwhile master limply confesses – only to be told, 'Then go and get me a glass of brandy, don't just stand there – get it!' Before that, as a bizarre prediction of the state of things to come, an ominously disquieting scene has been enacted. The two men, alone in the house, play a wild game of hide-and-seek in which ornaments are smashed on the staircase in a fit of infantilism encouraged by the servant, who resembles a cat preying on a foolishly trusting mouse.

In the final sequence the film falters, seeming to strive for another dimension which it fails to reach and which seems almost superfluous. Losey stated that he viewed the story as a modern Faustian allegory, in which case the final orgiastic scene seems lacking in diabolic Mephistophelean overtones. Barrett's calculated drive for supremacy turns abruptly and unconvincingly into a manic urge for meaningless destruction; uncharacteristically, he is shown wielding his power in a manner that could never serve his own interests, in a

scene whose texture is at variance with all that has gone before.

Dirk Bogarde, from his first bland appearance in his immaculate professional uniform of pork-pie hat, spotted tie and tasteful dark overcoat and leather gloves, gives a remarkable performance, and James Fox as his victim is equally superb. The women are less well-served with material: the blatant attempts of Tony's fiancée to bring Barrett to heel by ridiculing him would have been more effective had Wendy Craig given the character a slightly more upper-class veneer, and it seems unlikely that Sarah Miles' flagrant baggage would have trapped even Tony into more than a casual misdemeanour and a fleeting embarrassment. But both actresses are good enough to serve and strengthen the sinister bond between the two men. Among the incidental pleasures of this rewarding film are some hilarious glimpses of the fossilized aristocracy (Susan's parents, as played by Catherine Lacey and Richard Vernon); even a cameo appearance by Pinter himself as a 'society man'.

DEREK PROUSE

On the death of his parents in Kenya, Tony – young, rich and upper-class – buys a Georgian house in Chelsea. Though smart from the exterior, the house is dilapidated within and Tony hires a manservant, Barrett (1), to run the establishment for him. This he proceeds to do superlatively well; the house is soon transformed into a haven of gleaming elegance. Tony, also, is impeccably ministered unto by Barrett, ever ready with a comforting aspirin or a warming foot-bath (2).

Susan, Tony's fiancée, is quick to realize that her own part in Tony's life is being usurped (3) and her resentment of Barrett's ascendancy over Tony flares into open warfare. Barrett counters this by installing a young girl,

Vera (whom he claims to be his sister), in the household as a temporary maid (4). Vera seduces Tony (5, 6), who later discovers she is, in fact, Barrett's girlfriend when he and Susan return home (7) to find that the servant and the maid have been making love in their master's bed. He dismisses them both.

He has become dependent on Barrett, however, and the house once more falls into wrack and ruin. A chance encounter in a pub (8) leads to Barrett's reinstatement. Tony is reduced to a pawn completely under Barrett's dominion (9). The house deteriorates into a squalid nightly rendezvous for orgies and general perversion (10) with Tony now hopelessly dependent on drugs (11).

3

4

Directed by Joseph Losey, 1963

Prod co: Springbok/Elstree (Warner-Pathé). **prod:** Joseph Losey, Norman Priggen. **sc:** Harold Pinter, from the novel by Robin Maugham. **photo:** Douglas Slocombe. **ed:** Reginald Mills. **art dir:** Richard Macdonald, Ted Clements. **cost:** Beatrice Dawson. **mus:** John Dankworth. **song:** 'All Gone', sung by Cleo Laine. **sd:** John Cox, Gerry Hambling. **sd rec:** Buster Ambler. **prod man:** Teresa Bolland. **ass dir:** Roy Stevens. **r/t:** 115 minutes. Premiere, Venice Film Festival, 3 September 1963.
Cast: Dirk Bogarde (*Barrett*), James Fox (*Tony*), Wendy Craig (*Susan*), Sarah Miles (*Vera*), Catherine Lacey (*Lady Mounset*), Richard Vernon (*Lord Mounset*), Ann Firbank (*society woman*), Doris Knox (*older woman*), Harold Magee (*bishop*), Alun Owen (*curate*), Jill Melford (*young woman*), Harold Pinter (*society man*), Derek Tansley (*head waiter*), Gerry Duggan (*waiter*), Brian Phelan (*Irishman*), Hazel Terry (*woman in big hat*), Philippa Hare (*girl in bedroom*), Dorothy Bromiley (*girl outside phone-box*), Alison Seebohm (*girl in pub*), Chris Williams (*coffee bar cashier*), John Dankworth (*band leader*).

7

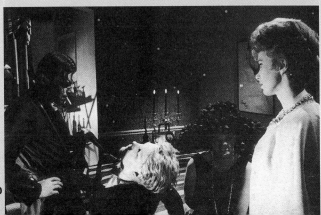

10

11

1

2

3

6

A LOVE CAUGHT IN THE FIRE OF REVOLUTION

Turbulent were the times and fiery was the love story of Zhivago, his wife... and the passionate, tender Lara.

METRO-GOLDWYN-MAYER PRESENTS A CARLO PONTI PRODUCTION

DAVID LEAN'S FILM OF BORIS PASTERNAK'S

DOCTOR ZHIVAGO

STARRING
GERALDINE CHAPLIN · JULIE CHRISTIE · TOM COURTENAY
ALEC GUINNESS · SIOBHAN McKENNA · RALPH RICHARDSON
OMAR SHARIF (AS ZHIVAGO) · ROD STEIGER · RITA TUSHINGHAM
SCREEN PLAY BY ROBERT BOLT · DIRECTED BY DAVID LEAN · IN PANAVISION® AND METROCOLOR

WINNER OF 6 ACADEMY AWARDS!

David Lean's film of *Doctor Zhivago* is at once an instance of old-style movie-making in the tradition of *Gone With the Wind* (1939) and the beginning of a new phase in the history of the epic. By the mid-Sixties the vogue for biblical epics had waned. The Roman Empire had indeed fallen and the financial debacle of *Cleopatra* (1963) effectively sealed the fate of the cloak and sandal spectaculars. That broad, sweeping canvas of history needed changing again and the Russian Revolution, with its explicit theme of the old order giving way to the new and its cinematic potential for blending costume drama with a more up-to-date historical theme, seemed an ideal proposition. When

the rights to Boris Pasternak's Nobel prize-winning novel were offered by producer Carlo Ponti to MGM, the film of *Doctor Zhivago* began to make economic sense, even in a Hollywood baffled at the loss of its own Midas touch.

When the project was begun, the book was high in the best-seller lists, the scandal by which the Soviet authorities had denied Pasternak permission to accept his prize was still fresh in people's minds, and David Lean – with the Oscar-winning *The Bridge on the River Kwai* (1957) and *Lawrence of Arabia* (1962) under his belt – was among the most bankable directors in the business.

Lean set up his production base

on a ten-acre site near Madrid airport, as Spain was proving more economical than Hollywood for the shooting of big-budget movies. Even so *Doctor Zhivago*'s original budget of $7.5 million was doubled by increased production costs.

In their meticulous re-creation of the Moscow streets (carefully altered to denote the passage of time) nearly eight hundred craftsmen worked for more than two years to create one of the most elaborate sets ever erected outside Hollywood. John Box, the production designer, had worked with Lean on *Lawrence of Arabia* as had the other key technicians.

Lean's casting reflected his preference for familiar faces such as Alec Guinness and Ralph Richardson, though there were people in Hollywood who felt that risks were being taken with the then little-known Omar Sharif and Geraldine Chaplin. Equally important to the director's conception was the authenticity of the film's many exterior scenes. Accordingly, the entire unit was moved to a location in Eastern Finland not far from the Russian border. Here, in temperatures of 30°C below zero, local people made daily appearances as extras in the re-staging of the great retreat from the Eastern Front, a scene which, like many in the movie, captured in the long shot of the Panavision 70

frame the epic nature of the narrative.

The first six months of *Doctor Zhivago*'s world-wide release proved that Hollywood could still make the old epic formula work: MGM were $18 million happier despite the lukewarm response of the critics. Reviewers, especially those in Britain, felt that Pasternak's 'difficult and elusive' novel had been betrayed and the much-repeated question seemed to be: 'How could an American studio film a Russian classic anyway?'.

The answer depended on what image of a Russian classic – and specifically what account of the Russian Revolution – would be widely acceptable to Western audiences. With the Cold War and the

8

52

Yuri Zhivago is in love with and later marries Tonya Gromeko (1), whose family brought him up after his parents died. While studying medicine in Moscow he meets and is attracted to Lara (2), the daughter of a dressmaker. When Komarovsky, her mother's lover, seduces and humiliates Lara, she shoots and wounds him at a party (3). Taking this action to be a gesture of political revolt in a climate of violent demonstrations (4), Pasha, a committed revolutionary, escorts Lara from the party (5) and they are later married.

During World War I, when Zhivago is working as a doctor at the front he again meets Lara who has become a nurse (6). Back in Moscow Zhivago finds the city transformed by the Revolution and himself under suspicion for the poetry he has published. Yevgraf, his half-brother and a Bolshevik police commissar (7),

urges Zhivago to flee Moscow with the family and stay at their country estate (8). Zhivago discovers that Lara is living nearby and he visits her frequently until his capture by Red Army partisans.

For a while Zhivago serves as a doctor but later deserts and makes his way to Lara's house. The Gromeko family have been deported to France and Zhivago and Lara elect to stay in Russia and live on the estate, where they enjoy a brief spell of happiness (9) before Komarovsky returns and persuades Lara to flee. Years later, still searching for Lara, Zhivago dies on a Moscow street and Lara disappears into a labour camp. Their daughter, however, has survived and is discovered by Yevgraf working on the construction of a hydro-dam. He completes the story of her parents for her (10).

Cuban Missile Crisis over, the new tone of East-West relations was characterized by the word 'thaw'. What better reflection of this mood than a warm and glowing love story set against the snowy wastes of icy, inhospitable Russia? When Lean cuts from Zhivago and Lara's love-making to a field of spring daffodils blooming after the long winter, the ideology of the film becomes most transparent – human values, such as love and passion, are represented as more enduring than political systems. In the same way, the 'survival' of Zhivago's artistic talent through his daughter is essential to the film's argument, even if the final shot of a rainbow over the newly completed dam stretches credibility into cliché.

For all the seductions of its setting and story, *Doctor Zhivago* has two potentially troublesome themes. The story turns on an adultery in which the two protagonists are allowed to indulge, and the outcome of the historical events is the modern Soviet state. What remains fascinating about the film is the way in which it negotiates these twin 'problems', first by stressing the poetic and artistic side of Zhivago's character which legitimizes his 'immorality', and second by focusing attention on a small group of wholesome individuals who are given added depth by being set against the drably-dressed and brutalized mass of Pasternak's people.

MARTYN AUTY

Directed by David Lean, 1965

Prod co: Carlo Ponti. **exec prod:** Arvid Griffen. **prod:** Carlo Ponti. **sc:** Robert Bolt, from the novel by Boris Pasternak. **photo** (Eastman Color, print by Metrocolor. Panavision 70): Freddie Young. **sp eff:** Eddie Fowlie. **ed:** Norman Savage. **art dir:** Terence Marsh, Dario Simoni. **cost:** Phyllis Dalton. **mus:** Maurice Jarre. **sd:** Winston Ryder. **2nd unit dir:** Roy Bossotti. **2nd unit photo:** Manuel Berenguer. **ass dir:** Roy Stevens, Pedro Vidal. **prod man:** Augustin Pastor, Douglas Twiddy. **r/t:** 193 mins.
Cast: Omar Sharif (*Yuri Zhivago*), Julie Christie (*Lara*), Geraldine Chaplin (*Tonya*), Rod Steiger (*Komarovsky*), Alec Guinness (*Yevgraf*), Tom Courtenay (*Pasha/Strelnikov*), Ralph Richardson (*Alexander*). Siobhan McKenna (*Anna*), Rita Tushingham (*the girl*), Jeffrey Rockland (*Sasha*), Tarek Sharif (*Yuri age 8*), Bernard Kay (*the Bolshevik*), Klaus Kinski (*Kostoyed*), Gérard Tichy (*Liberius*), Noel Willman (*Razin*), Geoffrey Keen (*medical professor*), Adrienne Corri (*Amelia*), Jack MacGowran (*Petya*), Mark Eden (*engineer at dam*), Erik Chitty (*old soldier*), Roger Maxwell (*Colonel*), Wolf Frees (*delegate*), Gwen Nelson (*female janitor*), Lucy Westmore (*Katya*), Lili Murati (*the train-jumper*), Peter Madden (*political officer*), Mercedes Ruiz (*Tonya age 7*).

20th CENTURY-FOX PRESENTS

RODGERS and HAMMERSTEIN'S

A ROBERT WISE Production

THE SOUND OF MUSIC

CinemaScope PICTURE AND COLOUR DE LUXE

Starring JULIE ANDREWS CHRISTOPHER PLUMMER

Co-starring RICHARD HAYDN with PEGGY WOOD, CHARMIAN CARR and ELEANOR PARKER as "The Baroness" THE BIL BAIRD MARIONETTES Associate Producer SAUL CHAPLIN Directed by Robert Wise

Music by Richard Rodgers · Lyrics by Oscar Hammerstein II · Additional words and Music by Richard Rodgers · Screenplay by Ernest Lehman

Production Designed by BORIS LEVEN · Produced by Argyle Enterprises Inc.

The Sound of Music is one of the most phenomenally successful movies in all cinema history: at the time of its release it dethroned *Gone With the Wind* (1939) as the cinema's box-office king, receiving numerous Academy Awards, including Best Picture and Best Director. This kind of commercial pedigree, though, merely added fuel to the fires of hatred of the many who regarded the picture as the very nadir of Western culture – insurmountable barriers being the picture-postcard scenery, the maudlin sentimentality of the plot, and the starchy wholesomeness of Julie Andrews.

Even when the stage version opened on Broadway in 1959, many thought it was dated, and the film certainly seemed curiously old-fashioned and sentimental, evoking the world of the classic MGM musical rather than such Sixties 'swingers' as *Sweet Charity* (1969) and *West Side Story* (1961). Nonetheless, concessions were made, in the form of a choice of directors associated with more 'realistic' forms. William Wyler was originally to direct, but *The Collector* (1965) seduced him away from the project and he was replaced by Robert Wise, famous for a line in bleak thrillers and for the neo-realist musical *West Side Story*. What mattered was that the film's essential optimism came at a time of cultural confusion and political unrest. It made a show of more 'eternal' values, and the irresistible image of brightly-clad Maria sitting against the hills strumming her guitar could appeal even to the growing consciousness of the new counter-culture.

Wise opens both *West Side Story* and *The Sound of Music* with powerful aerial shots which introduce the larger forces overshadowing the lives of the protagonists: skyscrapers and looming mountains tower over their worlds. Maria is first seen as a tiny figure from this God-like perspective, but the 6

exhilarating aerial shot rushes in on her as the affirmation of hopes and dreams in the title song suddenly fills the screen. Music thus becomes, as in the classic musical, a natural form of expression of optimism in the face of personal and social turmoil. And the music expands against Alpine settings, the natural images aspiring to a Romantic, almost Wordsworthian conception of nature.

Wise's decision to use actual locations could have resulted in a charming prettiness, but he and editor William Reynolds utilize them to stunning effect as music and setting are ultimately wed by snappily orchestrated images. 'Do-re-mi', for instance, shifts with *musical*, not *geographical*, logic from hilltop, to town, ending in a

---

Directed by Robert Wise, 1965

Prod co: Argyle Enterprises. **prod:** Robert Wise. **assoc prod:** Saul Chaplin. **sc:** Ernest Lehman, based on the stage musical by Richard Rodgers and Oscar Hammerstein II from the book by Howard Lindsay, Russel Crouse. **photo** (DeLuxe, Todd-AO): Ted McCord. **add photo:** Paul Beeson. **sp eff:** L. B. Abbott, Emil Kosa Jr. **ed:** William Reynolds. **art dir:** Boris Leven. **set dir:** Walter Scott, Ruby Levitt. **cost:** Dorothy Jenkins. **mus dir:** Irwin Kostal. **chor:** Marc Breaux, Dee Dee Wood. **sd:** Murray Spivack, Bernard Freericks. **2nd unit sup:** Maurice Zuberano. **ass dir:** Ridgeway Callow. **r/t:** 172 minutes.

Cast: Julie Andrews (*Maria*), Christopher Plummer (*Captain von Trapp*), Eleanor Parker (*the Baroness*), Richard Haydn (*Max Detweiler*), Peggy Wood (*Mother Abbess*), Charmian Carr (*Liesl*), Heather Menzies (*Louisa*), Nicholas Hammond (*Friedrich*), Duane Chase (*Kurt*), Angela Cartwright (*Brigitta*), Debbie Turner (*Marta*), Kym Karath (*Gretl*), Anna Lee (*Sister Margaretta*), Portia Nelson (*Sister Berthe*), Ben Wright (*Herr Zeller*), Daniel Truhitte (*Rolf*), Norma Varden (*Frau Schmidt*), Gil Stuart (*Franz*), Marni Nixon (*Sister Sophia*), Evadne Baker (*Sister Bernice*), Doris Lloyd (*Baroness Ebberfield*).

park, skilfully sustaining a visual equivalent to the music's rhythmic momentum with the use of bike and trap rides, camera movement and length of shot.

The film's star, Julie Andrews, was introduced to cinema audiences in *Mary Poppins* (1964) but rocketed to overnight fame in the role of Maria. The character she played, a novice nun who leaves her order to 'discover' herself in the world outside, embodies principles seen as the antithesis of both the ordered life of the Abbey and the stratified world of the Trapp household – both of which are more thoroughly elaborated than the hastily sketched-in threat of Nazism. She has an open, spontaneous, fresh approach to life, as exemplified by the music, with its natural imagery, which she brings into the Trapp home. Maria creates a new 'harmony' here by re-introducing the Captain to his own children on the simple basis of friendship. At the film's conclusion, they leave the ancestral home and values behind

and are seen amidst nature, eternally, as it were, climbing every mountain in search of a new ideal.

In the decade of *Sex and the Single Girl* (1964) and *Prudence and the Pill* (1968), Maria comes over as far less dated a heroine in her rejection of such ascribed female roles as an angel or the perfect symbol of an ordered home. The film, however, ends evasively by uniting the family as the true enemy of fascism.

The extraordinary success of the film proved a one-off in several ways. It remained, for example, a kind of musical that no-one was fast to emulate. Fox once again teamed Andrews with director Wise in the lavish *Star!* (1968), but it was an unmitigated box-office flop. The phenomenon of *The Sound of Music* was unrepeatable, the adaptability of its star unthinkable; the musical looked forward to rock, disco and Bob Fosse, and Andrews' career has failed to flourish in films for her husband, Blake Edwards.

MARTIN SUTTON **1**

Maria, a postulant in Austria's Nonnberg Abbey, spends more time adoring nature and the outside world than she should (1). To help adjust her priorities, the Mother Abbess suggests Maria is sent to work as a governess for Captain von Trapp, a widower, and his seven children.

On the way to the Captain's mansion she is apprehensive, but the thought of freedom excites her (2). The Captain, however, proves to rule his household in a military manner (3), and Maria works hard to bring warmth and music into the home. She returns to the shelter of the Abbey when she feels herself falling in love with the Captain, who is planning to marry the sophisticated Baroness Schrader (4).

But the Mother Abbess encourages her to leave the order and pursue her new feelings (5). Upon her return to the family (6), the Captain breaks off his engagement to the Baroness when he realizes that it is Maria he loves (7), and they are married in the Abbey.

The Nazis summon the Captain to return to the navy, but his anti-fascist beliefs force him to plan an escape for the family. During a local music festival, the Trapps leave the stage, elude the brown shirts by hiding in the Abbey, and cross over the mountains for the neutrality of Switzerland (8).

No modern film, not even *Doctor Zhivago* (1965), embodies so universal a charge of romantic passion as does *Elvira Madigan*. Portrayed in a limpid, impressionist style, this most aching of tragedies has the timeless beauty of a great picture or musical composition – and indeed part of *Elvira Madigan*'s enduring appeal lies in its use not only of Mozart's Piano Concerto No. 21, but also of Vivaldi's Violin Concerti.

Bo Widerberg, Swedish cinema's arch sociologist and poet *manqué*, did not intend the film to be merely a saccharine romance about a nineteenth-century army officer and his beloved tightrope artiste: 'Perhaps the time will come when one can choose more than a single life', says the married Sixten to his mistress. This is the voice of Widerberg bringing the movie into a social context. Today there is that freedom of choice for which Sixten yearned; love is no longer outlawed.

However, the ramifications of *Elvira Madigan* extend still further. It is a film about barriers – social, mental and emotional. Class differences still exist in Sweden and Widerberg suggests time and again in this elegiac film how monetary and family discrepancies prevent human beings from making contact with each other. Sixten and Elvira have committed many more breaches of convention than merely falling in love. He, a Count, has abandoned his army-career, wife and children, to mix with a girl from the circus milieu. The emotional pressures are sickeningly tangible and most apparent at such moments as the arrival of Sixten's friend from the regiment or Elvira's reunion with some Italian musicians. Compromise is impossible for this doomed couple and they must accept the consequences of their flight.

Sixten can see nothing beyond the blade of grass directly before his eyes. 'But without grass, the world would be nothing,' he tells his friend. It is this intensity that places the film above superficially similar attempts to crystallize pleasure – *Le Bonheur* (1965, *Happiness*) or *Un Homme et une Femme* (1966, *A Man and a Woman*).

Caught in a landscape of breathtaking wonder and beauty, Sixten and Elvira rapidly pass through all the familiar stages of passion: the childish ecstasy and teasing, the discovery of each other's strengths and weaknesses, the panic, the dull acknowledgment of failure and futility. Suicide is the only means by which their love may be sustained. However, the couple are left not on a note of melancholy so much as on one of recaptured elation as Elvira's ecstatic face is 'frozen' on the screen.

Widerberg does not strive for a conventional articulation of emotion, *Elvira Madigan* was based on a 25-page script without dialogue. Thommy Berggren and Pia Degermark were told their lines just three minutes before the shooting

Directed by Bo Widerberg, 1967
Prod co: Europa Film. **sc:** Bo Widerberg. **photo** (Eastman Colour): Jörgen Persson, Helena Englesson. **ed:** Bo Widerberg. **mus:** Mozart's Piano Concerto No. 21, extracts from Vivaldi's Violin Concerti. **sd:** Sven Fahlén. **ass dir:** Kalle Boman. **prod man:** Waldemar Bergendahl. **r/t:** 95 minutes. Stockholm premiere, 24 April 1967.
Cast: Pia Degermark (*Elvira Madigan*), Thommy Berggren (*Count Sixten Sparre*), Lennart Malmer (*Kristoffer*), Nina Widerberg (*little girl*), Cleo Jensen (*cook*).

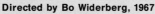

of each scene. Feelings are transmitted less through words than through a shy glance, a twisting of the fingers, a slump of the shoulders. At the very peak of their happiness a bottle of wine is knocked over and spreads out across the snow-white cloth as if it were a premonition of catastrophe for the lovers. Sexual desire and its fulfillment are conveyed as Sixten and Elvira undress each other in silhouette, followed by a cut to the cook opening the windows at dawn the next morning.

As so often in Nordic films, the climate dictates the mood and pattern of the piece. The glorious summer gives way to rain and harsh winds as Elvira and Sixten set out on their last journey. The colour is breathtaking and the whole of *Elvira Madigan* radiates an intimate bliss, a sensual affection for natural light and objects.

Elvira and Sixten cannot relax for a moment without being watched by

the local Danish folk: their ardour, as much as their social class, makes them conspicuous in the bucolic environment; money grows scarce; Sixten shaves off his moustache. In these ways Widerberg communicates the surreptitiousness that must accompany every clandestine affair.

Pia Degermark won the Best Actress Award at the 1967 Cannes Festival, and the film attracted large audiences in Britain and the United States. The public saw in these ill-fated lovers something of the determined individualism of Bonnie Parker and Clyde Barrow, whose story was evoked that same year in Arthur Penn's *Bonnie and Clyde*.

The greatness of *Elvira Madigan* is its ability to gaze, more or less in close-up, at the magic and tragedy of romance. The spectator feels almost ashamed at witnessing such personal intimacy.

PETER COWIE **5**

Elvira Madigan is a young tightrope artiste (1) who is passionately in love with a married Swedish army officer, Count Sixten Sparre (2). Together the lovers flee to Denmark and for one short summer they revel in the throes of a marvellous affair, wandering along the seashore (3) and through the meadows (4).

Then, as money runs out, the atmosphere changes. Sixten is tracked down by a friend and reproached for having deserted his family. Quarrels begin to develop as Elvira and Sixten try to live off the woods by eating berries and mushrooms. Eventually they arrive at a tacit agreement to commit suicide.

Concealing a gun in a picnic basket, Sixten and Elvira wander along the dunes and into the woods for a final breakfast (5). As Sixten takes out the gun he finds that he cannot shoot Elvira in cold blood (6). However, the sight of a butterfly fluttering above the grass revives memories of happier, more carefree days, and as Elvira opens her hands to release the insect, Sixten musters his courage and fires . . . Seconds later he turns the gun on himself, while the face of his inamorata, frozen by the camera in a moment of ecstasy, remains on screen (7).

Stills 2, 5 and 6 are production shots taken during the filming

the ultimate trip

2001: A SPACE ODYSSEY

MGM PRESENTS THE STANLEY KUBRICK PRODUCTION

2001: A Space Odyssey contains perhaps the boldest and most celebrated cut ever conceived by a film-maker; it is the biggest jump-cut in history, spanning four million years. The cut occurs after an ape has thrown a bone – which he used to kill another ape – into the sky. The camera follows the bone's ascent until, inevitably, it succumbs to gravity and begins to fall. As it does so, the film cuts to a space-craft, the creamy colour of bone, drifting across the screen to the strains of 'The Blue Danube'.

Directed by Stanley Kubrick, 1968
Prod co: MGM. **prod:** Stanley Kubrick. **sc:** Stanley Kubrick, Arthur C. Clarke, from the short story *The Sentinel* by Arthur C. Clarke. **photo** (Metrocolor, Super Panavision, presented in Cinerama): Geoffrey Unsworth, John Alcott. **sp eff:** Stanley Kubrick, Wally Veevers, Douglas Trumbull, Con Pederson, Tom Howard. **ed:** Ray Lovejoy. **art dir:** John Hoesli. **prod des:** Tony Masters, Harry Lange, Ernie Archer. **cost:** Hardy Amies. **mus:** Richard Strauss, Johann Strauss, Aram Khachaturian, György Ligeti. **sd:** Winston Ryder. **ass dir:** Derek Cracknell. **r/t:** 141 minutes. Washington premiere, 1 April 1968.
Cast: Keir Dullea (*David Bowman*), Gary Lockwood (*Frank Poole*), William Sylvester (*Dr Heywood Floyd*), Daniel Richter (*moonwatcher*), Douglas Rain (*voice of HAL 9000*), Leonard Rossiter (*Smyslov*), Margaret Tyzack (*Elena*), Robert Beatty (*Halvorsen*), Sean Sullivan (*Michaels*), Frank Miller (*mission controller*), Penny Brahms (*stewardess*), Alan Gifford (*Poole's father*).

There are three 'expository' captions in *2001*, added at a late stage in the production, but no caption separates the ape sequence from the one which describes Dr Floyd's journey to the moon. Clearly, there is an important aesthetic consideration – a caption would have destroyed the impact of the cut – but it suggests that the two sequences are identical, divided by time but not in meaning. History simply repeats itself.

Both sequences hinge on the discovery of a monolith, those inscrutable slabs which propel man further along the evolutionary path. The apes are saved from extinction and are transformed into carnivores and sentient killers. The dispute at the waterhole has its modern equivalent in the Orbiter Hilton, when Floyd and some Russian scientists probe each other over drinks. The apes fondle the monoliths and later – eons later – Floyd repeats the action on the moon. The grunts and shrieks of the apes become the meaningless jargon and empty platitudes of the spacemen.

This narrative symmetry is rigorously pursued throughout *2001*, but always in visual terms. The patterns of oblongs (continually opening doors, the monoliths, the computer's terminals) and circles (planets, spacecraft) are insistent and in apparent opposition, preparing for the moment when the oblong monolith creates a circle in the form of the embryo. The physical beings in the film undergo a similar process – the apes have wrinkled faces, like old men, and the youthful astronaut, Bowman, ages at the end until he too acquires a disturbingly ape-like appearance, transformed by the monolith into a child not yet emerged from the womb. Conversely, the super-intelligent computer, HAL 9000, regresses to childhood at the moment of death.

This technique turned *2001* into a critical controversy and a cult. The ending was discussed and analysed in countless articles, whilst audiences, primarily young, flocked repeatedly to the film that was billed on its first re-issue as 'The Ultimate Trip'.

When the film was first announced as *Journey Beyond the Stars* no one, probably not even Stanley Kubrick, could have foreseen the three year's work, the escalating budget or the 'non-verbal experience', as Kubrick called it, that materialized. It began almost as a documentary, but as filming progressed, acquiring its Homeric title in 1966, Kubrick's conception changed significantly, eliminating all explicatory material and most of the dialogue. The novel of *2001*, by co-scenarist Arthur C. Clarke, was based on the original screenplay and explained everything in detail. Inevitably, Clarke's novel was misguidedly used as a key to decipher Kubrick's film.

3

5

6

9

10

The film marked the refinement of special effects and it remains unsurpassed as a technical achievement. It was made against a background of cultural turbulence – the youth and drug culture, post-Kennedy neurosis, Vietnam – and seemed to embody an entire generation's mystical yearnings through its psychedelia and metaphysical optimism.

2001 was made during a period of great upheaval at MGM, whose president at the time backed Kubrick's vision in the face of prolonged opposition. The gamble paid off and Kubrick's consequent lionization led to increasing introspection and misanthropy. *A Clockwork Orange* (1971), *Barry Lyndon* (1975) and *The Shining* (1980) might be regarded as the 'missing caption' between the bone and the spacecraft, the chilling products, perhaps, of a recalcitrant monolith or a HAL 9000 computer.　　ADRIAN TURNER

The Dawn of Man. Families of apes struggle for survival in the wilderness (1), foraging the sparse vegetation for food. One day a family discovers a monolithic object on their territory which they examine excitedly. Apparently under the monolith's influence, an ape uses a bone as a weapon, killing grazing animals for food. During a dispute at a waterhole an ape is cudgelled to death. Dr Heywood Floyd flies to the moon (2), where he visits an excavation site and examines a monolith which emits a powerful radio signal (3).

Jupiter Mission: 18 Months Later. Aboard the spacecraft *Discovery* (4), Poole and Bowman fly to Jupiter. Three other crew members are in artificial hibernation and a talking computer HAL 9000 controls the electronic systems. Poole and Bowman gradually suspect HAL of treachery (5) and as Poole repairs the outer radio antenna

HAL arranges his death. Bowman retrieves his friend's body (6) but whilst he is outside *Discovery* HAL kills the rest of the crew by cutting off their life-support systems. Bowman abandons Poole's body when HAL forces him to re-enter the spacecraft through an emergency airlock. Bowman disconnects HAL's circuits (7) and as a result he receives a pre-recorded video message in which Mission Control tells him of the discovery on the moon and that the monolith's radio signal was aimed at Jupiter.

Jupiter and Beyond the Infinite. As Bowman approaches Jupiter in a space 'pod' he experiences a hallucinatory journey through time and space (8), arriving in an ornate suite of rooms (9). He watches himself pass into decrepit old age (10) and as he lies in bed he is confronted by a monolith which transforms him into an embryo floating in space.

easy Rider

'A man went looking for America and couldn't find it anywhere' announced the posters that advertised *Easy Rider*. It was a fitting summation of the low-budget film which defied Hollywood traditions and, at the same time, grossed more money than many of the lavish productions of the same year. Although this was the first film either of them had directed, Dennis Hopper and Peter Fonda sold their product to Columbia for $355,000: it went on to take more than $20 million at the box-office.

With its spontaneity and sincerity and its roots firmly in Sixties culture, *Easy Rider* established a new trend in movies: the 'road' film. Hollywood was quick to catch on to the idea of films whose characters had no history and travelled for no apparent reason; the journey becoming a metaphor for life, and the adventures on the road an allegory of man's search for himself. It also fostered a new taste in motorcycles – the Harley-Davidson 'Chopper'.

Wyatt and Billy set off across America on their own personal odyssey looking for a way to lead their lives. On the journey they encounter bigotry and hatred from small-town communities who despise and fear their non-conformism.

and it is these who finally kill off the dreams that they do not understand. Although Wyatt and Billy also discover people attempting 'alternative life-styles' who are resisting this narrow-mindedness, there is always a question-mark over the future survival of these drop-out groups. The gentle hippy community who thank God for 'a place to stand' are living their own unreal dream. The rancher and his Mexican wife are hard-pushed to make ends meet. Even LSD turns sour when the trip is a bad one. Death comes to seem the only freedom. It is significant that, in the final scene, the solitary burning bike remains: Wyatt's spirit lives on.

The film's essential philosophy is controversial, if unspoken. Nonetheless, it is eloquently articulated through the pulsating rock soundtrack, the emphasis on dope-smoking as a common aspect of life, the loving shots of the rolling scenery as they ride across America, and the equation of motorbikes with freedom rather than with the hooliganism of *The Wild One* (1953) and its successors. It was, perhaps, the only film to portray the new culture from within that culture itself.

Easy Rider also works on a

number of mythic and symbolic levels. Hopper had recently become engrossed in Thomism (a philosophical system based on the teachings of Thomas Aquinas) and indeed, it has been seen as the story of a modern prophet . . . from the difficulties of getting hotel rooms to the final violent 'crucifixion'. Another interpretation might suggest that Wyatt and Billy are the drop-out versions of their famous Western namesakes, reversing the traditional journey by travelling east on motorbikes rather than west on horses: a rejection of the old Hollywood and its myths and dreams. One further ironical aspect of this view is that Henry Fonda – Peter's father – once played Wyatt Earp in *My Darling Clementine* (1946). But there are no heroes in *Easy Rider*; identification is stimulated by the mood of the film rather than by characters who have no history and are therefore ideal subjects for mythical legend.

The filming process also rejected Hollywood traditions, as the crew themselves followed the same eastward journey, picking up their actors in the towns they passed through – often improvising action and dialogue. One dramatic scene in the diner, for instance, was done in this way: the locals were told that Hopper and Fonda were sexual

child-molesters, and the customers reacted appropriately vehemently. One actor not recruited *en route* was Jack Nicholson, who gained fame and an Oscar nomination for his portrayal of the liberal lawyer who drowns his uncertainties in alcohol.

In itself, *Easy Rider* is a work full of contradictions – including the fact that Hopper took time off from shooting to appear in *True Grit* (1969), a film with almost the opposite philosophy. Wyatt and Billy finance their journey from the proceeds of a cocaine sale, a hard drug which does not have the same idealistic connotations as marijuana. After their disappointment at the Mardi Gras, Wyatt acknowledges to Billy that 'we blew it'. There had to be another way to search for their freedom, one that was not betrayed from the start.

But despite its depressing message – that America has become so corrupt and bigoted that even those who try to find ways of escaping the system will be destroyed by it – the film is an exhilarating celebration of the alternatives that the Sixties offered. *Easy Rider* seems to say that if anyone blew it, it was America for not allowing a new and challenging, freer, more personal culture to exist.

SALLY HIBBIN

Directed by Dennis Hopper and Peter Fonda, 1969
Prod co: Pando Company/Raybert Productions. **exec prod:** Bert Schneider. **prod:** Peter Fonda. **assoc prod:** William Hayward. **sc:** Peter Fonda, Dennis Hopper, Terry Southern. **photo** (Technicolor): Laszlo Kovacs. **sp eff:** Steve Karkus. **ed:** Donn Cambren. **art dir:** Jerry Kay. **songs:** 'The Pusher', 'Born to Be Wild' by Steppenwolf, 'I Wasn't Born to Follow' by The Byrds, 'The Weight' by The Band, 'If You Want to Be a Bird' by The Holy Modal Rounders, 'Don't Bogart Me' by Fraternity of Man, 'If Six Was Nine' by The Jimi Hendrix Experience, 'Let's Turkey Trot' by Little Eva, 'Kyrie Eleison' by The Electric Prunes, 'Flash, Bam, Pow' by The Electric Flag, 'It's Alright Ma (I'm Only Bleeding)', 'Ballad of Easy Rider' by Roger McGuinn. **sd:** Ryder Sound Service. **prod man/ass dir:** Paul Lewis. **r/t:** 95 minutes.
Cast: Peter Fonda (*Wyatt*), Dennis Hopper (*Billy*), Antonio Mendoza (*Jesus*), Phil Spector (*connection*), Mac Mashourian (*bodyguard*), Warren Finnerty (*rancher*), Tita Colorado (*rancher's wife*), Luke Askew (*stranger*), Luana Anders (*Lisa*), Sabrina Scharf (*Sarah*), Sandy Wyeth (*Joanne*), Robert Walker (*Jack*), Robert Ball, Carman Phillips, Ellie Walker, Michael Pataki (*mimes*), Jack Nicholson (*George Hanson*), George Fowler Jr (*prison guard*), Keith Green (*sheriff*), Hayward Robillard (*cat man*), Arnold Hess Jr (*deputy sheriff*), Buddy Causey Jr, Duffy LaFont, Blase M. Dawson, Paul Guedry Jr, Suzie Ramagos, Elida Ann Hebert, Rose LeBlance, Mary Kaye Hebert, Cynthia Grezaffi, Collette Purpera (*customers in café*) Toni Basil (*Mary*), Karen Marmer (*Karen*), Cathi Cozzi (*dancing girl*), Thea Salerno, Ann McLain, Beatriz Monteil, Marcia Bowman (*hookers*), David C. Billodeau, Johnny David (*men in pick-up truck*).

After the successful completion of a cocaine sale in California (1), Wyatt (known as Captain America) and Billy stash their money in Wyatt's fuel-tank and set off on their motorbikes across America (2) in order to reach New Orleans in time for Mardi Gras. Unable to get a hotel room because of their

long hair and general unkempt appearance, they sleep out in the open. A couple who are trying to make a living from their small ranch give them a meal. Continuing on the road, they pick up a hitch-hiker who takes them to a hippy community that he is heading for (3). The life-style

1

2

3

4

6

7

seems idyllic, but after a brief stay Wyatt and Billy move on.

When they arrive at a diner in a small town, they are insulted by the local rednecks as weirdo degenerates (4). They are arrested on some minor pretext by the local sheriff and thrown into jail where they meet George Hanson, a liberal alcoholic lawyer (5). He gets them out and decides to join them on their trip to New Orleans. The next night, when the three of them are sharing a joint (6), their camp is attacked and George is clubbed to death by the sheriff he had antagonized.

Wyatt and Billy ride on (7). They pick up two girls from the House of Blue Lights, the brothel that George dreamed of visiting, and go to the Mardi Gras, which seems plastic and dull. In a cemetery they all take LSD and share a bad trip (8).

Wyatt and Billy decide to carry on riding to Florida. On the road, a jeep driver thinks he'll have a little fun with the two of them (9) and takes a pot shot at Billy, whom he accidentally shoots in the stomach (10). Wyatt rides off for help, but the driver returns and deliberately shoots him. In the closing image his bike lies burning on the tarmac.

9

10

Directed by Steven Spielberg, 1977
Prod co: Phillips/Columbia/EMI. **prod:** Julia Phillips, Michael Phillips.
assoc prod: Clark Paylow. **sc:** Steven Spielberg. **photo** (Metrocolor,
Panavision): Vilmos Zsigmond, William A. Fraker, Douglas Slocombe. **col:**
Robert M. McMillian. **add photo:** John Alonzo, Laszlo Kovacs, Steve Poster.
sp photo eff: Richard Yuricich, Dave Stewart, Robert Hall, Don Jarel, Dennis
Muren. **anim sup:** Robert Swarthe. **anim:** Harry Moreau, Carol Boardman,
Eleanor Dahlen, Cy Didjurgis, Tom Koester, Bill Millar, Connie Morgan.
visual eff sup: Steven Spielberg. **sp photo eff sup:** Douglas Trumbull. **sp
photo eff co-ord:** Larry Robinson. **project co-ord:** Mona Thal Benefiel. **eff
unit project man:** Robert Shepherd. **video tech:** 'Fast' Eddie Mahler. **ed:**
Michael Kahn. **art dir:** Dan Lomino. **design:** Joe Alves, Phil Abramson,
Matthew Yuricich, George Jensen, Carlo Rambaldi. **sp mech eff:** Roy
Arbogast, George Polkinghorne. **mech design:** Dom Trumbull, John
Russell, Fries Engineering. **electronics design:** Jerry L. Jeffress, Alvah J.
Miller, Peter Regla, Dan Slater. **models:** Gregory Jein, J. Richard Dow, Jor
Van Kline, Michael McMillen, Kenneth Swenson, Robert Worthington.
mus/mus dir: John Williams. **songs:** 'Chances Are' by Al Stillman, Robert
Allen, sung by Johnny Mathis; 'When You Wish Upon a Star' by Leigh
Harline, Ned Washington; 'The Square Song' by Joseph Raposo; 'Love
Song of the Waterfall' by Bob Nolan, Bernard Barnes, Carl Winge, sung by
Slim Whitman. **cost:** Jim Linn. **makeup:** Bob Westmoreland. **titles:** Dan
Perri. **sd:** Gene Cantmessa, Buzz Knudson, Don MacDougall, Robert
Glass. **Dolby sd sup:** Steve Katz. **sd eff:** Frank Warner, Richard Oswald,
David Horton, Sam Gemette, Gary S. Gerlich, Chet Slomka, Neil Burrow.
tech adv: Dr. J. Allen Hynek. **sp consultants:** Peter Anderson, Larry
Albright, Richard Bennett, Ken Ebert, Paul Huston, David M. Jones, Kevin
Kelly, Jim Lutes, George Randle, Jeff Shapiro, Rourke Engineering. **tech
dialogue:** Colin Cantwell. **stunt co-ordinator:** Buddy Joe Hooker. **ass dir:**
Chuck Myers, Jim Bloom. **r/t:** 135 minutes.
Cast: Richard Dreyfuss (*Roy Neary*), François Truffaut (*Claude Lacombe*),
Teri Garr (*Ronnie Neary*), Melinda Dillon (*Jillian Guiler*), Bob Balaban
(*David Laughlin*), J. Patrick McNamara (*project leader*), Warren Kemmer-
ling (*Wild Bill*), Roberts Blossom (*farmer*), Philip Dodds (*Jean Claude*), Cary
Guffey (*Barry Guiler*), Shawn Bishop (*Brad Neary*), Adrienne Campbell
(*Silvia Neary*), Justin Dreyfuss (*Toby Neary*), Lance Henriksen (*Robert*),
Merrill Connally (*team leader*), George DiCenzo (*Major Benchley*), Amy
Douglass, Alexander Lockwood (*implantees*), Gene Dynarski (*Ike*), Mary
Gafrey (*Mrs Harris*), Norman Bartold (*Ohio Tolls*), Josef Sommer (*Larry
Butler*), Rev Michael J. Dyer (*himself*), Roger Ernest (*highway patrolman*),
Carl Weathers (*military policeman*), F. J. O'Neil (*ARP project member*), Phil
Dodds (*ARP musician*), Randy Hermann, Hal Barwood, Matthew Robbins
(*returnees from Flight 19*), David Anderson, Richard L. Hawkins, Craig
Shreeve, Bill Thurman (*air traffic controllers*), Roy E. Richards (*Air East
pilot*), Gene Rader (*hawker*), Eumenio Blanco, Daniel Nunez, Chuy Franco,
Luis Contreras (*federales*), James Keane, Dennis McMullen, Cy Young,
Tom Howard (*radio telescope team*), Richard Stuart (*truck dispatcher*), Bob
Westmoreland (*load dispatcher*), Matt Emery (*support leader*), Galen
Thompson, John Dennis Johnston (*special forces*), John Ewing, Keith
Atkinson, Robert Broyles, Kirk Raymond (*dirty tricks*).

Riding high on the success of *Jaws*
(1975), Steven Spielberg began his
ambitious project – initially entitled
'Watch the Skies' – with full studio
backing. He constructed an enormous set in an airplane hangar in
Mobile, Alabama, while shooting
certain outdoor scenes in a section
of Indiana desert land reminiscent
of Jack Arnold's locations in *It
Came From Outer Space* (1953) and
Tarantula (1955). Over a year was
spent shooting and re-shooting
scenes on various other international locations with the help of
some top cinematographers. These
sequences jigsawed together for
two versions, the first demanded by
an impatient Columbia, released in
1977, and the second – Spielberg's
authorized version – released three
years later.

Although the *Special Edition*
(1980) contains additional scenes,
the overall effect of the two films is
the same. Both are wonderful, brilliantly constructed science-fiction
drama featuring complex special
effects which are enhanced by
Spielberg's single-minded, all-
American, all-Hollywood vision. It
is a mammoth spectacle, as grip-
ping as Hitchcock, as magical as
Disney's early animated features,
and as humanely optimistic as the
best of the Sixties television series
The Outer Limits (1963–65).

The story is presented from three
simultaneous viewpoints: that of
the innocent child and his dis-
traught mother, of an intrigued
electrical engineer, and of a group
of scientists led by François Truffaut playing in his first American
movie. Everything revolves around
five or six breathtaking set-pieces;
the narrative intercuts between
these 'close encounters', excitingly
revealing the clues which lead to
the moving climax when the extra-
terrestrials come to rest on Devil's
Tower. Superbly edited throughout,
the film moves at an extraordinary
pace, teasing the audience with
constant references to the other
beings as Lacombe and his UFO
investigators discover the secret of
the five musical tones – a signal
continuously broadcast from outer
space.

In the first sighting is encapsu-
lated all the success of *Close Encounters of the Third Kind*: around
the curve of the road come three
multicoloured, gyrating shapes at
incredible speed but slow enough
to be in full view of witnesses and
the audience. By shooting the special effects in 70mm and the rest in
35mm, which is then blown up to
70mm, the quality of the print is
consistent so that the spacecraft
look completely real. It is the immaculate special effects, integrated so perfectly with the heart-
stopping narrative, which are the
true stars of *Close Encounters*. The
final sequence – the arrival of the
mothership on Devil's Tower – is as
startling as Cecil B. DeMille's part-
ing of the waves in *The Ten Commandments* (1956). Anyone would
find it difficult not to believe that this
great citadel in the sky, twice as
high as the mountain, really exists.

Unlike the swashbuckling
heroics of that other high-budget,
cosmic adventure movie *Star Wars*
(1977, dir. George Lucas), the ef-
fectiveness of *Close Encounters*
lies in our ability to believe that
beyond the stars superior powers
are benevolent and caring. In those
closing moments the audience is
allowed the kind of emotional par-
ticipation not felt in cinemas since
Judy Garland walked over the rainbow and Dumbo flew: perfect esca-
pism for our troubled times.

STEPHEN WOOLLEY

**Lost on the road while trying to
establish the cause of a massive
power-cut, Roy Neary sees a set
of bright lights approaching.
Instead of passing straight by, the
intense rays rise above his truck
(1), and immediately there is a
loss of all gravitational force in
his cab.**

**In another part of the same
black-out a young boy awakes to
find the entire house in bizarre
confusion; all the electrical
appliances have switched
themselves on. Amused and
amazed, he runs into the night
pursued by his fearful mother,
and mysteriously appears at the
edge of a hill-top road where Roy,
Jillian and the boy witness three
of the alien spacecraft.**

**Spurred on by newspaper and
television reports, interested
people turn up for these sightings
(2). Meanwhile, a group of
scientists led by Claude Lacombe
has found evidence in other
continents that a certain musical
pattern can be linked with the
aliens' efforts to communicate.**

**Jillian's son is invisibly
kidnapped by the extra-
terrestrials (3), and Roy alienates
his own family by building a clay
model of the visions he has seen
of a flat mountain (4). As soon as
he realizes, along with Jillian,**

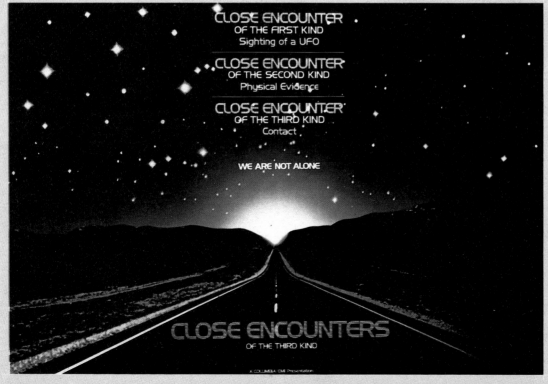

CLOSE ENCOUNTER
OF THE FIRST KIND
Sighting of a UFO

CLOSE ENCOUNTER
OF THE SECOND KIND
Physical Evidence

CLOSE ENCOUNTER
OF THE THIRD KIND
Contact

WE ARE NOT ALONE

CLOSE ENCOUNTERS
OF THE THIRD KIND

A COLUMBIA-EMI Presentation

1

2

3

4

5

6

that the model in his living room is the Devil's Tower in Wyoming and that the aliens want them to be there, he and Jillian race across country.

On arrival they find everything cordoned off by Lacombe (5) and the military who have simulated a nerve-gas scare. All the unwelcome humans drawn there are rounded-up for interrogation (6), but Roy and Jillian escape.

An exciting chase culminates in the discovery of a colossal runway, a giant electronic board covered with coloured strips, and a powerful musical keyboard. All their former paranoia is calmed by this sight, and their weird obsessions and premonitions now seem crystal clear.

A fleet of dancing, whooshing, neon-lit spaceships precede the landing of the huge mothership. Communication between the scientists and the craft is initiated by the playing of the five mystical notes, and culminates in an extra-terrestrial duet. Roy eventually enters the mothership surrounded by the aliens (7) – their embryonic features clear and their intentions obviously harmless. With sadness Lacombe and his team watch the friendly visitors leave (8). From a vantage point, Jillian and her son see the craft move off (9).

7

8

9